DELPHI

ARCHAEOLOGICAL GUIDE

ADAM EDITIONS

DELPHI

ARCHAEOLOGICAL
GUIDE

ΔΕΛΦΟΙ

Oh, thou! in Hellas deemed of heavenly birth,
Muse! formed or fabled at the minstrel's will!
Since shamed full oft by later lyres on earth,
Mine dares not call thee from thy sacred hill:
Yet there I've wandered by thy vaunted rill;
Yes! sighed o'er Delphi's long deserted shrine,
Where, save that feeble fountain, all is still;
Nor mote my shell awake the weary Nine
To grace so plain a tale - this lowly lay of mine.

(Lord Byron, from *Childe Harold's Pilgrimage*)

CONTENTS

The south-eastern corner of the temple of Apollo.

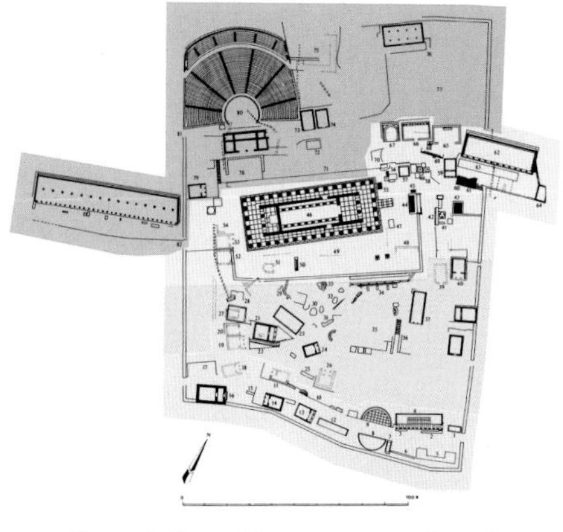

Ground plan of the sanctuary of Apollo.

Griffin from the decoration of a bronze cauldron (7th cent. BC).

Contents

The Athenian treasury (c. 530-490 BC).

The charioteer from the dedication of the tyrant of Gela (475-450 BC).

Statue of Dionysus (340-330 BC).

The village of Castri at the beginning of the "Big Excavation".

Prologue

Delphi is often mentioned in ancient Greek literary sources, but its actual location was discovered in the 15th century by Cyriacus, a tradesman from Ancona, who read the name of the city on inscriptions found in the area. From the 18th century onwards several travellers visited the place seeking the monuments mentioned by ancient writers, mainly Herodotus and Pausanias. Systematic excavations started at Delphi only in 1891, when an agreement was reached between Greece and France to begin the so-called 'Big Excavation' under the direction of the archaeologist Th. Homolle. The expropriation and removal of the village of Castri, which was built above the archaeological site, proved to be necessary for the beginning and continuation of the excavations. In 1903 the Delphi museum was inaugurated and a new period of excavations begun with the co-operation of the Greek Archaeological Service and the French Archaeological School. The monuments at the site were reconstructed and preserved between 1938 and 1942. Today, research continues and, despite the extensive excavations carried out in the past, Delphi has still many secrets to reveal.

The study and identification of most architectural remains and small objects found *in situ* is based on the reading of inscriptions and ancient texts. Of great importance is the contribution of Pausanias who visited the sanctuary in the 2nd century AD and included it in his *Description of Greece*, a detailed report of his travel around the country. However, the large quantity of the material forced Pausanias to be selective and thus not to mention several of the offerings he saw at Delphi. Therefore, despite its value, the work of Pausanias should be cautiously used; not only the omission of several monuments but also the fact that the direction followed by the author is not always clearly indicated suggest that the text should be treated with caution. Other writers, such as Herodotus (486-423 BC) and Plutarch (46-126 AD) - the latter had actually served a twin priesthood at the sanctuary - also inform us about Delphi but they refer mainly to matters concerning the cult of Apollo and the role of his oracle, without, however, neglecting to comment on the most impressive monuments.

These are the main sources used by archaeologists for the identification of the remains representing the glory of a panhellenic sanctuary. However, even today, several questions remain open and require further investigation. Delphi is a fruitful site for research and the picture changes constantly with new discoveries.

The following pages reveal several of the secrets buried in the past under the modern village of Castri. A brief discus-

View of the temple of Apollo and the theatre.

sion of the cult of Apollo and the significance of his oracle is followed by a visit to the archaeological site, which spreads over five areas (see p. 150-151): the sanctuary of Athena Pronaia, the Gymnasium, the Castalia spring, the sanctuary of Apollo and the Stadium- and a description of the objects exhibited in the museum. Finally, the chronological tables and the glossary can be used as reference. To conclude, the influence of the spirit of Delphi in modern thought and literature is briefly discussed in the Epilogue.

Delphi and the cult of Apollo

Zeus sent off from Olympus two eagles in opposite directions to discover the centre of the world. The birds finally met at Delphi, which in antiquity was considered to be the omphalos (navel) of the earth. The city of Delphi belongs to the county of Phocis and overlooks to the south the valley of the river Pleistus which spreads between the foothills of the mountains of Parnassus and Cirphi. Delphi is bounded on three sides by vertical cliffs, called the Phaedriades, and is an idyllic site where the green of trees and plants dominates the landscape. It gives an excellent view towards the imposing bulk of the neighbouring mountain tops and the sea at Itea. The modern village of Itea is the ancient Cirrha, the port of Crisa (the modern village of Chrisso), where those who approached the sanctuary of Apollo by sea disembarked.

The Delphic oracle is mostly known today for its activity during the Classical period. However, written sources and archaeological finds reveal that the area was inhabited from the Mycenean period (14th-11th century BC). The most important finds dated in this period are fragments of pottery, architectural remains (found in 1990 under the temple of Apollo), and clay statuettes. Regrettably the number of such finds is limited and thus neither their interpretation nor the location of places for cult practices is secure. Therefore, although it is certain that Delphi was inhabited in this period, it cannot also be argued that its importance as a cult centre was already established.

Attic cup, c. 480 BC. Apollo with lyre.

Finds dated to the so-called 'Dark Ages' (11th-9th century BC) are also limited. Characteristic is a group of bronze male figurines, most probably representing Apollo himself.

Extensive building activities, which began in the sanctuary in the Geometric and the Archaic periods and reached a peak in the Classical period, confirm that in the 8th century BC Delphi was already developing as a panhellenic cult centre. The temples and the monuments dedicated to Apollo are described later on, while myths referring to the establishment of Apollo's cult at Delphi as well as to the operation of the oracle are discussed in this section.

The *Homeric Hymn to Apollo* portrays the god in his childhood determined to found an oracle, which would enable him to reveal the decisions of his father Zeus. Apollo travels from one place to another in order to choose the right location for his oracle. Finally, he settles in the foothills of Parnassus, where he lays the foundations for his temple after killing the female dragon, who was guarding the sacred fountain in the area (*Homeric Hymn to Apollo*, 214-304 and 356-544). To serve him as priests,

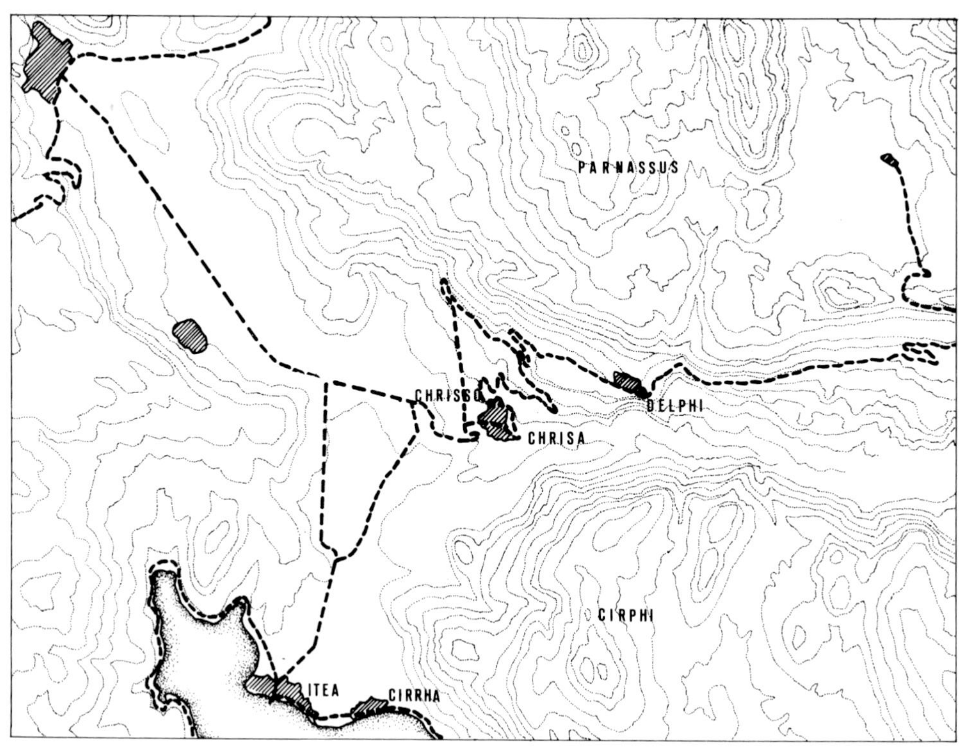

The area around Delphi.

he selected a group of Cretan merchants travelling in the Cretan Sea; the god, transformed into a dolphin, changed the destination of their ship and brought them to Delphi.

In the Classical period Apollo was not thought to be the founder of the oracle, but the successor of its previous owners. Aeschylus (*Eumenides*, 1ff) mentions that the oracle originally belonged to the goddess of Earth, Gaia; Themis, her daughter, succeeded her and then passed it over to her sister Phoebe. Later, Phoebe offered it to Apollo as a present for his birth and that is how the god acquired the title Phoebus. According to Euripides (*Iphigenia in Tauris*, 1947-1953) Apollo managed to succeed Gaia at Delphi, after killing the Python, the male dragon guarding her oracle. Finally, Pausanias (X,5,5-7) names as Apollo's predecessors both Gaia and Poseidon.

The discovery of a sanctuary dedicated to Gaia (see p. 44-45, no. 29) and the altar of Poseidon inside the cella of Apollo's temple may be considered as indications of respect towards the predecessors of the Delphic oracle. However, apart from Gaia and Poseidon, other deities were also venerated in the *temenos* of Apollo: an altar dedicated to Hestia has been found in the cella of Apollo's temple, while excavated material suggests that Heracles and Hermes may have been worshipped at the Gymnasium. An inscription mentions Hermes as sharing the temple of Apollo Pythius. A sanctuary in the honour of Neoptolemus has also been discovered, and finally it is attested that Antinous was deified at Delphi after his death in AD 130.

In addition, the cult of Dionysus was of major importance in Apollo's sanctuary. According to Plutarch (*Moralia,* 388E-F), Dionysus and his followers had to settle in Delphi for three months every winter. On a calyx crater by the Cadmus Painter dated around 420 BC, Apollo is shown shaking hands with Dionysus, a gesture sealing the agreement between the two gods. The fact that the deities are surrounded by satyrs probably suggests that the scene shows Dionysus being welcomed by Apollo for his temporary stay at Delphi. This incident is related to Apollo's punishment for killing the Python, which we mentioned above. Apollo, in order to expiate this murder, was obliged to go either to the valley of Tempe in Thessaly (Plutarch, *Moralia*, 293 C) or to Sicyon (Pausanias, II,7,7). This event was commemorated in a festival called the 'Septeria', which took place every eight years and during the ceremony the dragon's death and the flight of Apollo were reconstructed.

Calyx crater by the Cadmus Painter. Apollo is shaking hands with Dionysus.

Another kind of worship at Delphi was focused on sacred stones. These were: the stone which was given by Rhea to Cronus instead of his child Zeus (see p. 61, no. 77), the stone of Leto (see p. 45, no. 32), the rock of the Sibyl (see p 45, no. 30), who delivered the oracles when Gaia was the dominant deity in the sanctuary, and Apollo 'agieus', a conical rock which was supposed to ward off evil and was usually placed outside the houses.

The most important stone was the omphalos of the Earth. It was conical in shape and was covered with the so-called *agrenon*, a material resembling a net, which was formed by continuous locks of hair rendered in relief. Stones of this type were often offered to Apollo and were meant to signify that Delphi was the centre of the earth.

To conclude, the sanctuary, primarily, belonged to Apollo who possessed knowledge of prophecy. However, the discovery of other cults on the site indicates that Delphi apart from being the oracle of Apollo was also a very significant cult centre of panhellenic and international appeal.

The Delphic Oracle

The person delivering the oracles of Apollo was a woman named the Pythia. Information concerning her identity is limited; it is only known that she was a woman of fifty who had abandoned all her family obligations. Plutarch (*Moralia*, 292E-F) mentions that, at the beginning, the Pythia delivered oracles once a year, the seventh day of the Delphic month Bysios, which was the day Apollo was born. Later, the increasing popularity of the oracle resulted in the proclamation of the seventh day of each month as prophecy day. In addition, during periods of greater demand, two women alternated in the position of the Pythia and a third was also available as a replacement.

In order to be able to receive the oracles of Apollo, the Pythia first had to purify herself at the Castalia spring. This procedure prepared her for entering the *adyton* of Apollo's temple. In the *Homeric Hymn to Apollo* the Pythia is described as transmitting Apollo's prophecies as she reaches the state of ecstasy by chewing laurel leaves. Pausanias (X,24,7) claims that the Pythia was inspired by the water of the sacred spring Cassotis, which flowed underground to emerge in the *adyton* of Apollo's temple; the traveller pictures the Pythia seated on the sacred tripod of Apollo as she recites his prophecies.

Worshippers requesting an oracle could only approach the god after going through a preparation stage, which was organised by the priests. According to Plutarch (*Moralia*, 435B-C, 437, 438) oracles could not be delivered unless the day was proved to be of good omen. For this purpose the priests presented a goat to Apollo and sprinkled it with cold water; if the animal shivered then the omen was good, the day was considered to be appropriate, and those who had the right to request an oracle were allowed to enter the temple. Priority was arranged by lot, although only the city of Delphi had the right to be served first. This privilege was called *promanteia* and could be granted temporarily to other cities as a gesture of honour. Having entered the temple worshippers were first obliged to offer a tribute to the god, which was a pie called *pelanos*. Next, they sacrificed sheeps or goats. It was only after this procedure was completed that they were allowed to enter the adyton of the temple, where the Pythia was seated.

The Pythia prophesied in a state of ecstasy. Therefore the words coming from her mouth were incomprehensible and had to be deciphered and interpreted by experienced priests, before being handed to the pilgrims. The famous double meanings of Delphic oracles gave to Apollo the epithet Loxias, which can be translated as the 'ambiguous interpreter'. The flexibility in interpreting the Pythia's words secured the infallibility of the oracle; in the event of complaints about unpredictable situations it could be claimed that the Pythia's sayings had been misunderstood by point-

The temple of Apollo (4th cent. BC).

ing to their other meaning. The oracles were delivered either orally or in writing and were sealed in cases where they were handed to a representative.
The Delphic oracle flourished during the Archaic and Classical periods. Divine predictions were always valuable both for everyday matters and for important public affairs concerning one or more cities. The Delphic oracle established a high reputation mainly around the 8th century BC, which should probably be associated with the development of colonization at the end of the 8th and the beginning of the 7th century BC. The strong religious bonds between the mother-cities and the colonies made it necessary for the former to consult the oracle before deciding on the location and time regarding the foundation of a colony. Despite the fact that in most cases the decision had already been taken, the cities sought divine approval for moral support before commencing such an expedition.
Gradually, the respectable reputation of Apollo's oracle spread not only around Greece, but also around the wider Eastern Mediterranean region. In the beginning, during the 8th century BC, most of the worshippers came from neighbouring cities to consult the oracle about founding a colony in South Italy and Sicily. During the 7th century BC, the reputation of the Delphic oracle had already reached the Aegean islands and Asia Minor. Herodotus gives an account of rich offerings from various places: Midas (I,14), the king of Phrygia, gave a very valuable throne as a present to the sanctuary; Gyges (I,13,1), the first king of Sardis, requested an oracle in 675 BC regarding the reinforcement of his throne, and Croesus (I,50), the king of Lydia, dedicated precious offerings to the oracle. In the 6th century BC Solon asked Apollo for an oracle concerning the consolidation of his laws and Cleisthenes asked the Pythia to choose the heroes who would give their names to the ten Athenian tribes. Finally, in the period of the Persian and the Peloponnesian wars, the oracle played an important role in the decisions taken by the adversaries.
The large number of votive offerings on the site provides evidence of the great appeal of the oracle, mainly in the 6th and 5th centuries BC. However, prominent and rich offerings dedicated by cities would not only have been thought of as pure expressions of gratitude to Apollo, but also as demonstrations of their own power and wealth. Among the most distinctive dedications were the so-called treasuries. They were small temple-shaped buildings, which most probably housed the necessary vessels and other equipment used for accommodating official representatives and delegates. A city had to be enjoying a period of political power and prosperity in order to be able to finance the expensive costs of constructing a treasury. The reasons, or better the motives, for dedicating a treasury, or any other offering to Delphi, were of various kinds: it might have been a request for expiation when a city had shown contempt towards the oracle, or an expression of gratitude for a victory, or the commemoration of an important event, as well as the demonstration of wealth and power. In spite of their nature, dedications would have, most certainly, been well noticed and appreciated in a sanctuary of panhellenic appeal which was visited by thousands of people every year.

The Athenian treasury.

A VISIT TO THE ARCHAEOLOGICAL SITE

A. THE SANCTUARY OF ATHENA PRONAIA

The sanctuary of Athena Pronaia, today known as Marmarias, is situated on the left of the road approaching Delphi from Arahova. In antiquity Athena, who was worshipped in this sanctuary, was known with the title 'pronaia', which can be translated as 'the goddess in front of the temple', or 'pronoia', which signifies the goddess of concern and anticipation. According to written testimonies, which unfortunately have not been confirmed by archaeological finds, other deities have also been worshipped in this sanctuary: Artemis and Aphrodite Epiteleia (the goddess bringing to fulfilment), Harmonia and Epitymbia.

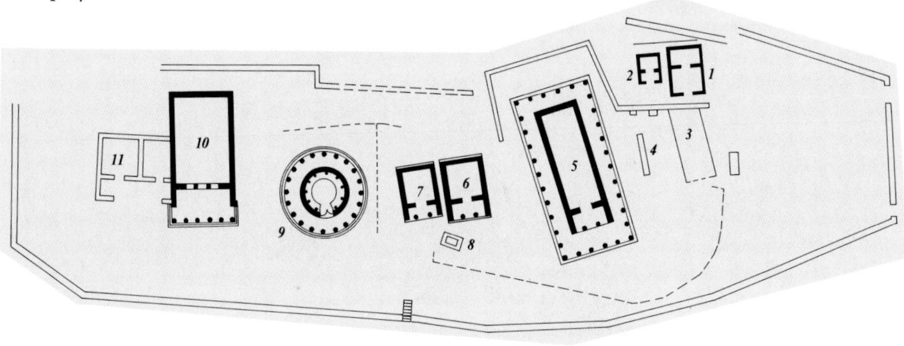

1-2. TWO SMALL TEMPLE-SHAPED BUILDINGS (OIKOI)
3. LARGE RECTANGULAR ALTAR
4. AREA OF THE ALTARS
5. TEMPLE OF ATHENA PRONAIA
6. DORIC TREASURY
7. TREASURY
8. BASE
9. THOLOS
10. TEMPLE OF ATHENA PRONAIA(?)
11. RECTANGULAR BUILDING

Approaching the site from the entrance located in the north-eastern corner of the peribolos we come across the architectural remains of the following buildings:

1-2. Two small temple-shaped buildings (oikoi)
They are enclosed by an enclosure wall, which might suggest that they belonged to the sanctuary of the local hero Phylacus. This sanctuary is mentioned by Herodotus (VIII, 39) together with another sanctuary dedicated to Autonous. Phylacus and Autonous were two local heroes who fought in the battle of Delphi against the Persians in 480 BC. However, some scholars believe that these sanctuaries were situated further to the north and thus interpret these two buildings as treasuries.

3. Large rectangular altar
Its foundations are contemporary with those of the temple of Athena dated in the 6th century BC (see below no. 5). Therefore, it has been argued that it may have been used for sacrifices in honour of the goddess herself.

4. Area of the altars
Most impressive are the foundations of a large altar dated in the Archaic period. Inscriptions, also found in the area, prove that smaller altars were dedicated to Athena Ergane, a goddess protecting work, Athena Soteira (Saviour), a deity guarding the safety of warriors, Zeus Polieus, the protector of cities, Hygieia, the goddess of health, and Eileithyia, the goddess of child-birth.

5. Temple of Athena Pronaia

Two architectural phases of the temple are discerned from the discovered remains. The first belongs to a small Doric temple made of limestone, which is dated around 650-630 BC. The second was a peripteral temple, with 6x12 columns on the peristyle, and a pronaos (porch) with two columns *in antis*. It was dated to the end of the 6th century BC and was either destroyed by the earthquakes that hit Delphi in 480 BC, or was deserted around 373 BC, when the latest temple of Athena was built (no. 10).

6. Doric treasury

This was a building made of limestone, with two columns *in antis* at the entrance and possibly a marble Doric frieze with metopes and triglyphs. It was built, most probably, just after the Persian Wars, around 475-470 BC, to commemorate the victory against the Persians.

7. Treasury

This also had two columns *in antis* at the entrance. Although the columns are of the Ionic order they are crowned by two capitals of peculiar shape, which have been thought to be Aeolic. It has been suggested that this building might have been the treasury of the Massaliotes (the people of Massalia (modern Marseilles), which was a colony of the city of Phocaea in Ionia), which is known to have been dedicated to Apollo around 540-500 BC.

Foundations of the treasuries (nos 6-7).

8. Base

It is believed that on this base stood the trophy which was erected by the city of Delphi to commemorate the repelling of the Persian army in 480 BC. According to Diodorus Siculus (XI,14,3-4), when the Persian forces had reached the shrine of Athena Pronaia and were attempting to invade the oracle, a great thunderstorm caused the fall of large rocks and as a result many of the enemy were killed and those who survived were compelled to flee. Thus, the Persians never succeeded in occupying Apollo's sanctuary.

9. Tholos

A round building dated around 380-370 BC. The architect, Theodorus of Phocaea (Vitruvius, VII, 12), had explored several innovative elements for its construction. Around the tholos is a circular peristyle with twenty Doric columns standing on a stepped platform (crepidoma). The columns carry a frieze with triglyphs and metopes decorated with an Amazonomachy and a Centauromachy (see p. 128-129, nos 1-3). The arrangement of the interior is similar: ten Corinthian columns, standing on a low step made of limestone, are placed parallel to the walls of the cella. The floor is covered with slabs made of black limestone apart from a white circle in the centre. The roofing system is particularly interesting: the roof of the cella was conical in shape and protruded above the roof of the peristyle.

The function of the tholos has been widely discussed, but the problem has not yet been solved. Pausanias (X,8,1-8) does not mention any circular building in his description of the sanctuary of Athena Pronaia. Assuming that the traveller did not consider it necessary to refer to its shape, the tholos could be identified with several buildings known to have existed in this sanctuary, such as the temple of Artemis, or one of the temples of Athena, or even the temple dedicated by the people of Thourioi to honour Boreus, the wind-god, who helped them to defeat the people of Syracuse in 379 BC. It might also be the *temenos* of Phylacus, which, as mentioned above (see p. 24), has not been securely located. Finally, it could also be interpreted as the arsenal which was renovated in the 3rd century BC and accommodated a panoply of the goddess Athena. It is hard to understand the purposes that a tholos could serve, because it is not a common type of building in ancient Greek architecture. The tholos of Epidaurus, dated around 360-320 BC, was probably dedicated to the worship of Asclepius. We can only be certain about the use of the tholos in the Athenian Agora, which was the dining place for the *prytaneis* (city officials). In general, however, the function of the tholos remains problematic, because

The tholos at the sanctuary of Athena Pronaia (no. 9).

Foundations of the temple of Athena (no 10).

neither written sources nor archaeological finds provide sufficient information.

10. Temple of Athena Pronaia(?)

At this point stood a Doric prostyle temple with six Doric columns on the front and a pronaos with two Ionic columns *in antis*. It is dated around the middle of the 4th century BC. Pausanias (X, 8, 6-7) describes in the pronaos of the temple a bronze statue dedicated by the city of Massalia (Marseilles), and a golden shield offered by Croesus from Lydia. This building was most probably the latest temple of Athena replacing the two earlier ones (see above no. 5).

11. Rectangular building

The latest temple of Athena (no. 10) was built above the eastern part of an earlier building. This is probably dated in the 5th century BC and its function is ambiguous: it may have been used as a residence for the priests, or as a dinning hall, or it might have been a temple with double cella, or even the marble workshop used for the tholos which became obsolete when the building was finished.

B. THE GYMNASIUM

The west exit of the sanctuary of Athena Pronaia takes us to the Gymnasium.
Every Greek city had a Gymnasium. It was usually located close either to the agora or to an important sanctuary. It was an educational institution for young men in antiquity, where their mind was trained by the *paidagogos* (teacher) and their body by the *gymnastes* (gym instructor). Specialised sciences, such as philosophy, rhetoric, astronomy etc., could also be taught at the Gymnasium. Classes were attended not only by young pupils, but also by adult citizens.
The Gymnasium of Delphi was an education centre for both locals and visitors, and was funded therefore by the Amphictyony and not by the city of Delphi. Inscriptions and votive offerings found *in situ* testify to the worship of Heracles and Hermes. It was built on the slopes of the mountain and extended on two levels supported by strong retaining-walls. On the lower level were the palaestra, a circular pool and the hot baths, while on the upper level were the so-called *xystos* and the *paradromis*.

General view of the Gymnasium.

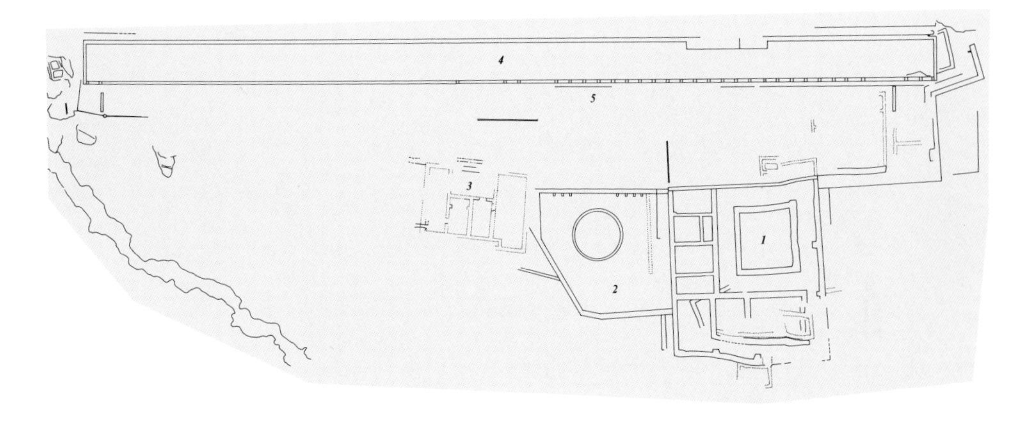

1. PALAESTRA
2. CIRCULAR POOL
3. BATHS
4. COVERED STOA–XYSTOS
5. OPEN TRACK–PARADROMIS

1. Palaestra
A square building with an interior courtyard surrounded by colonnades, with eight columns on each side, and rooms at the back. The palaestra was a meeting-place for men, where they could exercise as well as attend entertaining and cultural events.

2. Circular pool
This is located between the palaestra and the hot baths (no. 3). It was a round water reservoir, 1.90m deep and 10m in diameter, which was supplied by water by the Castalia spring (see p. 30-31). It was large enough to be used both for swimming and relaxing.

3. Baths
These were built in the Roman period, around AD 120, and provided rooms for hot baths.

4. Covered stoa - *xystos*
This was a long, narrow stoa situated on the upper level of the Gymnasium. It was roofed so that it could be used by runners for training during the winter, when the weather did not allow exercising in the open air. The name *xystos* signified that the soil on this track was always smooth and flat. The preserved bases once belonged to a row of Ionic columns standing along the façade of the stoa and dated to the Roman period. In earlier periods the front of the building was arranged with eighty-three Doric columns supporting a frieze with triglyphs and metopes.

5. Open track - *paradromis*
In front of the *xystos* was a long and narrow surface of flat soil, which was used for the training of runners in the open air. The ancient Greek word can be translated as 'place for taking the air', most probably meaning a locale for entertainment, walking and breathing fresh air.

C. THE CASTALIA SPRING

Crossing the road outside the Gymnasium we reach the Castalia spring.
Pausanias (X,8,9) relates the name of the spring either to a woman from Delphi or to a man named Castalius, and describes its water as pleasant for drinking and bathing. It is reported that the priests serving Apollo washed every morning at Castalia, as well as the pilgrims visiting the sanctuary. The spring had several architectural phases. It must have been in use since the Archaic period, judging from the testimony of Herodotus (VII,39), who places the sanctuary of the local hero Autonous close to Castalia. The earliest level of the spring, which is dated around 600 BC, has been reconstructed as a paved square courtyard with benches along three of the walls and with four spring sources, in the shape of lion heads, conveying water on the fourth wall. The Castalia which is described by Pausanias is located to the north of the Archaic spring and was most probably the latest architectural phase. It was a monumental construction carved into the rock and dated to the 1st century BC. It has been reconstructed with a rectangular basin flanked by two smaller rooms for storing water. It was built of limestone and had an interior paved courtyard with niches on three walls holding votive offerings, while on the fourth wall were seven bronze lion heads serving as outlets for the water. During the Turkish occupation the spring was transformed into a little church of Saint John. In 1899 the church was demolished and replaced by an icon in a niche carved into the rock and a shrine on the right side of the road between Arahova and Delphi.

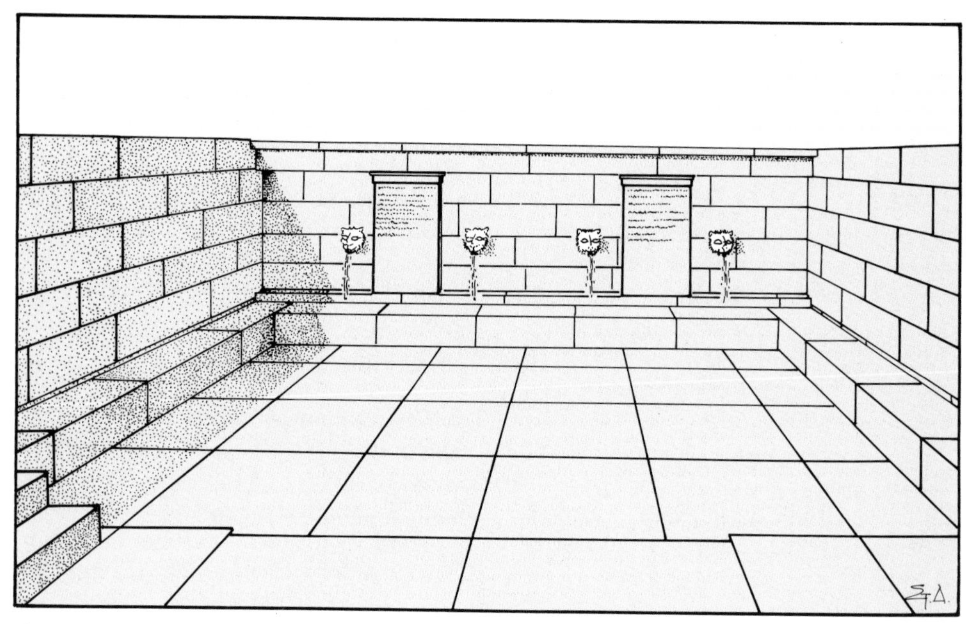

Reconstruction of the Archaic Castalia spring.

Right: The architectural remains of the Castalia spring which was carved into the rock (1st cent. BC).

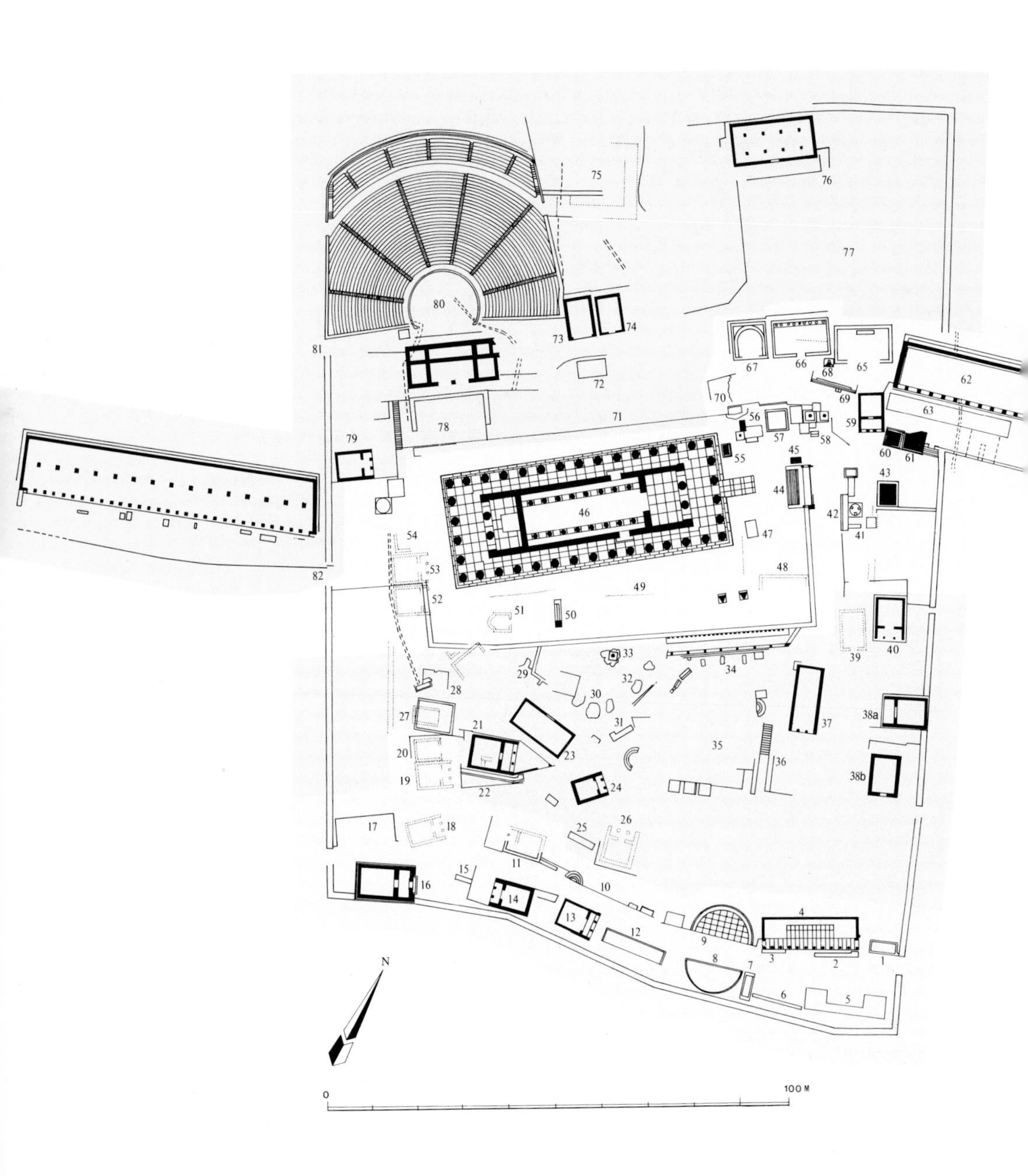

Ground plan of Apollo's sanctuary.

D. THE SANCTUARY OF APOLLO

At the entrance of the sanctuary, between the museum and the Castalia spring, is the beginning of the Sacred Way. This path, which was paved in the Byzantine period, runs across the *temenos* of Apollo. The remains in front of the entrance once belonged to a Roman forum (agora) with stoas constructed with Ionic colonnades at the front and stores at the back. Today in this area stand the bases of Roman statues.

The sanctuary is spread over the slope of the mountain. Therefore, the location of the buildings was inevitably dictated by the terrain and consequently did not follow any architectural plan. As we climb up the slope we walk along the Sacred Way which leads to the temple of Apollo. In antiquity this path was crowded with votive offerings, the tokens of respect and appreciation paid by various cities to the honoured god. These monuments are briefly described in the following pages and are numbered according to the attached plan of the site.

1. DEDICATION OF THE PEOPLE OF CORCYRA - BRONZE BULL
2. OFFERING OF THE ARCADIANS - BRONZE STATUES OF GODS AND HEROES
3. DEDICATION OF THE ACHAEAN CONFEDERACY - STATUE OF PHILOPOEMEN
4. RECTANGULAR BASE
5. SPARTAN OFFERING - BRONZE STATUES
6. ATHENIAN OFFERING - BRONZE STATUES
7. OFFERING OF ARGOS - BRONZE STATUE OF THE TROJAN HORSE
8. ARGIVE OFFERING - BRONZE STATUES OF THE SEVEN AGAINST THEBES AND THE EPIGONOI
9. ARGIVE MONUMENT - BRONZE STATUES OF MYTHICAL KINGS
10. FOUNDATIONS OF NICHES AND BASES OF VOTIVE OFFERINGS
11. FOUNDATIONS OF A TREASURY
12. OFFERING OF TARAS - BRONZE STATUES OF WOMEN AND HORSES
13. TREASURY OF SICYON
14. SIPHNIAN TREASURY
15. OFFERING OF THE LIPARAEANS - BRONZE STATUES
16. TREASURY OF THEBES
17. RECTANGULAR NICHE FOR AN OFFERING WITH STATUES
18. "BOEOTIAN" TREASURY
19. TREASURY
20. ARCHAIC TREASURY
21. ATHENIAN TREASURY
22. VOTIVE OFFERING OF THE ATHENIANS FOR THE VICTORY AT THE BATTLE OF MARATHON
23. BOULEUTERION
24. TREASURY OF CNIDUS (?)

25-26. FOUNDATIONS OF TREASURIES (?)

27. SANCTUARY OF ASCLEPIUS
28. WATER SPRING OR FOUNTAIN OF ASCLEPIUS
29. SANCTUARY OF GAIA,
30. ROCK OF THE SIBYL
31. BOEOTIAN OFFERING
32. STONE OF LETO
33. NAXIAN SPHINX
34. ATHENIAN STOA
35. THE HALOS
37. CORINTHIAN TREASURY
38. a,b. FOUNDATIONS OF BUILDINGS
39. FOUNDATIONS, ARCHAIC TREASURY
40. TREASURY OF THE CITY OF ACANTHUS AND BRASIDAS
41. TRIPOD DEDICATED FROM THE SPOILS OF THE BATTLE OF PLATAEA
42. OFFERING OF TARAS
43. MONUMENT OF THE RHODIANS - GILDED CHARIOT OF HELIOS
44. OFFERING OF THE CHIANS - ALTAR OF APOLLO
45. DEDICATION OF THE CONFEDERACY OF THE AETOLIANS - STATUE OF EUMENES II
46. THE TEMPLE OF APOLLO
47. BASE FOR THE STATUE OF AEMILIUS PAULUS
48. FOUNDATIONS OF A TEMPLE-SHAPED BUILDING (OIKOS)

49 FOUNDATIONS

50. SPRING
51. APSIDAL BUILDING

52, 53, 54. TEMPLE-SHAPED BUILDINGS

55. ATHENIAN OFFERING - PALM-TREE AND GILT IMAGE OF ATHENA
56. OFFERING OF THE CONFEDERACY OF THE AETOLIANS - STATUE OF PRUSIAS II
57. PERHAPS THE BASE OF THE STATUE OF APOLLO "SITALKAS"
58. OFFERINGS OF THE DEINOMENIDS - GOLDEN TRIPODS
59. FOUNDATIONS OF AN ARCHAIC TREASURY
60. BASE OF THE STATUE OF ATTALUS I
61. BASE OF THE STATUE OF EUMENES II
62. STOA OF ATTALUS I
63. PEDESTAL FOR THE OFFERINGS OF ATTALUS I
64. TEMPLE-SHAPED BUILDING
65. TEMENOS OF NEOPTOLEMUS
66. MONUMENT OF DAOCHUS
67. NICHE OF A VOTIVE OFFERING
68. POSSIBLY THE LOCATION OF THE "COLUMN OF THE DANCING GIRLS"
69. POSSIBLY A PEDESTAL FOR THE OFFERINGS OF THE CORCYREANS
70. CASSOTIS SPRING (?)
71. PLACE OF DISCOVERY OF THE BRONZE CHARIOTEER
72. "POTEIDANION" (?)

73, 74. TEMPLE-SHAPED BUILDINGS

75. INCOMPLETE BUILDING
76. LESCHE OF THE CNIDIANS
77. "STONE OF CRONUS"
78. EXEDRA OF CRATERUS
79. TREASURY
80. THEATRE
81. OFFERING OF CNIDUS - POSSIBLE LOCATION OF THE STATUE OF DIONYSUS
82. STOA OF THE AETOLIANS

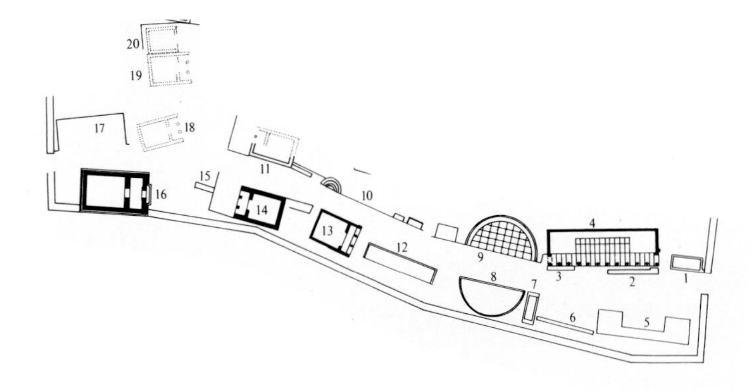

1. DEDICATION OF THE PEOPLE OF CORCYRA - BRONZE BULL
2. OFFERING OF THE ARCADIANS - BRONZE STATUES OF GODS AND HEROES
3. DEDICATION OF THE ACHAEAN CONFEDERACY - STATUE OF PHILOPOEMEN
4. RECTANGULAR BASE
5. SPARTAN OFFERING - BRONZE STATUES
6. ATHENIAN OFFERING - BRONZE STATUES
7. OFFERING OF ARGOS - BRONZE STATUE OF THE TROJAN HORSE
8. ARGIVE OFFERING - BRONZE STATUES OF THE SEVEN AGAINST THEBES AND THE EPIGONOI
9. ARGIVE MONUMENT - BRONZE STATUES OF MYTHICAL KINGS
10. FOUNDATIONS OF NICHES AND BASES OF VOTIVE OFFERINGS
11. FOUNDATIONS OF A TREASURY
12. OFFERING OF TARAS - BRONZE STATUES OF WOMEN AND HORSES
13. TREASURY OF SICYON
14. SIPHNIAN TREASURY
15. OFFERING OF THE LIPARAEANS - BRONZE STATUES
16. TREASURY OF THEBES
17. RECTANGULAR NICHE FOR AN OFFERING WITH STATUES
18. "BOEOTIAN" TREASURY
19. TREASURY
20. ARCHAIC TREASURY

As we enter the sanctuary, to the right of the Sacred Way, we encounter:

1. Dedication of the people of Corcyra - bronze bull

Only the limestone base, on which the bull stood, has been preserved. The monument was the work of the sculptor Theopropus from Aegina. According to Pausanias (X,9,3), it was dedicated around 480 BC as a gesture of appreciation for the Delphic oracle which brought to the city of Corcyra a catch of large fish.

2. Offering of the Arcadians - bronze statues of gods and heroes

On the inscribed base, which has been found *in situ*, stood nine bronze statues of gods and local heroes (see Pausanias X,9,5-6). The monument was dedicated from the spoils of the victorious invasion of Laconia by the Arcadians, with the assistance of Epaminondas in 370-369 BC.

3. Dedication of the Achaean Confederacy - statue of Philopoemen

The inscription on the pedestal testifies that the bronze statue was dedicated by the Achaean Confederacy to the memory of Philopoemen just after his death, in 183 BC. Philopoemen was a general of the Achaeans who was honoured for his bravery at the battle of Mantineia (207 BC), which resulted in the defeat of the Spartan hoplites and the death of the Spartan tyrant Machanidas.

4. Rectangular base

The remains suggest that here stood a large rectangular exedra with a Doric colonnade on the façade. The archaeological evidence is not sufficient to enable us to identify this building.

To the left of the Sacred Way, as we enter the sanctuary, are:

5. Spartan offering - bronze statues
Only parts of the limestone base have been preserved. The purpose of this dedication was to commemorate the victory of Sparta at Aigospotamoi (404 BC), which resulted in the end of the Peloponnesian War. Pausanias (X,9,7-11) describes the statues of deities such as Poseidon, Zeus, Apollo, and Artemis as well as statues of the Dioscouroi – the demigods who were honoured as local heroes in Sparta – together with the statue of the admiral Lysander and other Spartans who fought in this naval battle.

6. Athenian offering - bronze statues
Part of the base, which in antiquity held sixteen bronze statues, can be seen today. According to Pausanias (X,10,1-2) the monument represented Athena, Apollo and the general Miltiades surrounded by ten Attic heroes. Three more statues were added to the group in the Hellenistic period. These were the statues of the Macedonians Antigonus and his son Demetrius, as well as the statue of Ptolemy I of Egypt, who were honoured by giving their names to three Athenian tribes (*phylae*). Pausanias reports that the monument was dedicated from a tenth (tithe) of the spoils gathered from the battle of Marathon (490 BC) and that it was made by Pheidias. However, it has also been suggested that the initiative for this dedication was taken by Cimon to honour his father, Miltiades, who died in 465 BC and had played a crucial role at the battle of Marathon.

7. Offering of Argos - bronze statue of the Trojan Horse
This monument was made by the sculptor Antiphanes. It was most probably dedicated from the spoils gathered when the Argives invaded the city of Thyrea, in 414 BC. Thyrea was situated at the border with Sparta and according to Thucydides (6,95) the motive for the invasion was to take revenge on Sparta for undertaking an expedition against Argos.

8. Argive offering - bronze statues of the Seven against Thebes and the Epigonoi
The foundations and bricks discovered here suggest that the monument might have been standing on a semi-circular inscribed base. Pausanias (X,10,3-4) describes the statues of the seven kings of Argos who supported Polynices in his claim to the throne of Thebes, against his brother Eteocles. The tragic end of this campaign is well known, as well as the failure of the descendants of the Argive kings to avenge the death of their fathers. The statues of the descendants (the Epigonoi) most probably stood on the same monument. This offering was the work of the sculptors Hypatodorus and Aristogeiton and was dedicated from the tenth (tithe) of the spoils from the victory of Argos over Sparta at the battle of Oenoe in the Argolid, in 456 BC.

Opposite monument no. 8, on the right side of the Sacred Way are:

9. Argive monument - bronze statues of mythical kings
A semi-circular exedra can be seen, which accommodated a large base holding approximately ten bronze statues. The inscription on the base identifies it as another offering of Argos made by the sculptor Antiphanes. According to Pausanias (X,10,5), the offering was supposed to commemorate the participation of Argos in the foundation of Messene by Thebes and Epaminondas, around 370 BC. The

statues portrayed the Argive family of Heracles, including the hero himself and his mother, Alcmene. The dedication of such a monument was supposed to emphasise the friendship developing between Argos and Thebes by promoting the figure of Heracles, a hero who was supposed to have his family roots in Argos and to have been born in Thebes.

To the west of the last offering of Argos (no. 9) are preserved:

10. Foundations of exedras and bases of votive offerings

11. Foundations of a treasury

The decrees concerning the city of Megara, which are inscribed on the retaining-wall in front of this building, suggest its possible identification with the Megarian treasury. Unfortunately, this particular treasury is not mentioned by Pausanias, probably because it had been destroyed before the middle of the 2nd century AD.

Opposite monuments numbered 10 and 11 are:

12. Offering of Taras - bronze statues of women and horses

On the upper surface of the base found here, the position of sixteen female riders arranged in groups of four can be traced. Pausanias (X,10,6) reports that it was the work of the sculptor Ageladas from Argos and mentions that the dedication was made from the spoils of the victory of the people of Taras (a Spartan colony in southern Italy) against their neighbours in the city of Metapontium. The monument should probably be dated to the first quarter of the 5th century BC.

13. Treasury of Sicyon

This was most probably built at the end of the 6th century BC and was dedicated by the oligarchic party to commemorate the overthrow of the tyranny of the Orthagoridae. The foundations discovered belong to a limestone building with two columns *in antis* at the entrance. Parts of two earlier buildings have been detected among the construction material: 1) a tholos, which most probably had a peristyle with thirteen columns and is dated around 580 BC, and 2) a 'monopteros' with a roofed colonnade. The latter probably accommodated the chariot of Cleisthenes, the tyrant of Sicyon, which won the first chariot race at the Pythian Games in 582 BC. The metopes exhibited in room IV of the museum belonged to this building (see p. 94-97, no. 4).

14. Siphnian treasury

This is situated on the left of the Sacred Way and its entrance faces west. The occasion for dedicating this Treasury was a Delphic oracle. Upon the discovery of the gold and silver mines on Siphnos Apollo demanded that a tenth of their revenues should be sent to Delphi. The people of Siphnos built the treasury and offered to the sanctuary a tenth of their annual revenues from the mines as an expression of gratitude for their wealth. A *terminus ante quem* for dating the treasury

Caryatid from the Siphian treasury (no. 14).

is around 524 BC, when Siphnos was destroyed. Although this event is confirmed by archaeological finds and is reported by ancient sources, the reasons that caused it are still not clear. According to Pausanias (X,11,2-3) the mines of Siphnos were destroyed by a heavy sea, when the Siphnians failed to keep their promise to Apollo. But Herodotus (III,57) mentions that Siphnos was ravaged by refugees who had rebelled against the tyrant Polycrates.
The Siphnian treasury was an Ionic building with innovative architectural elements: first, the entablature on its façade was carried by two Caryatids in antis, instead of columns, and secondly the entablature and the architectural sculpture were made of marble from the island of Paros. The use of marble, which was an expensive material, as well as the rich decoration of the building, clearly demonstrates the wealth of Siphnos in this period. The sculpture of the treasury is exhibited in room III of the museum, which we will visit later on (see p. 80-91).

As we continue walking along the Sacred Way, in the area extending to our left, the remains of several buildings have come to light which cannot be securely identified:

15. Offering of the Liparaeans - bronze statues

Pausanias (X,11,3-4) mentions that the people of Lipara, who were colonists from Cnidus, dedicated statues to commemorate a naval victory against the Etruscans, who were most probably pirates. However, some scholars identify the foundations of a rectangular exedra (no. 17) as the location of this offering and believe that this monument (no. 15) was a treasury.

16. Treasury of Thebes

According to Pausanias (X,11,5) this was built on the occasion of the victory of the Theban general Epaminondas over Sparta, at the battle of Leuctra in 371 BC. The preserved foundations indicate that the building had a pronaos and a cella. Its façade was decorated with a Doric frieze, which was not carried on columns, but on a wall with a door at the centre.

17. Rectangular exedra for an offering with statues

This might have been the location of the offering of the Liparaeans mentioned above in no. 15. However, the remains do not allow a secure identification for this monument.

18. 'Boeotian' treasury

This name is conventional. The preserved foundations belonged to a Doric building dated around the end of the 6th century BC. Inscribed stones have also been found in the area, which were probably parts of the inscription mentioning the names of the donors, without, unfortunately, providing any information on the building itself.

19. Treasury

This was contemporary with the treasury of the Athenians (see below no. 21), but we do not know who dedicated it.

20. Archaic treasury

To the north of building no. 19 are the foundations of one more treasury which, judging from its construction techniques, should be dated around the 6th century BC. It has been suggested that this might be the treasury dedicated by the city of Potidea (see Pausanias, X,11,5).

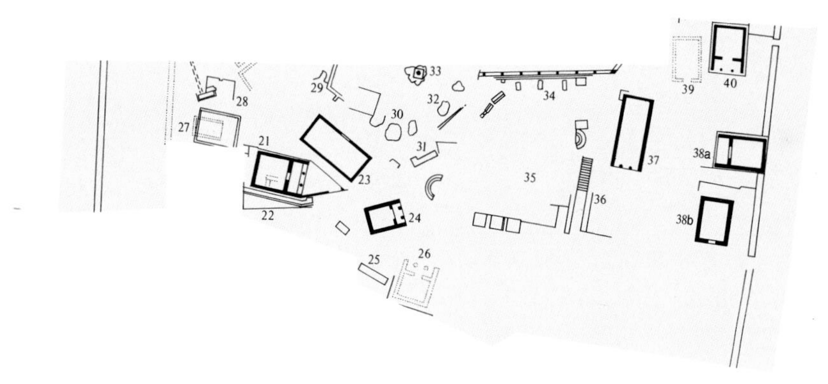

21. ATHENIAN TREASURY
22. VOTIVE OFFERING OF THE ATHENIANS FOR THE VICTORY AT THE BATTLE OF MARATHON
23. BOULEUTERION
24. TREASURY OF CNIDUS (?)
25-26. FOUNDATIONS OF TREASURIES (?)
27. SANCTUARY OF ASCLEPIUS
28. WATER SPRING OR FOUNTAIN OF ASCLEPIUS
29. SANCTUARY OF GAIA
30. ROCK OF THE SIBYL
31. BOEOTIAN OFFERING
32. STONE OF LETO
33. NAXIAN SPHINX
34. ATHENIAN STOA
35. THE HALOS
37. CORINTHIAN TREASURY
38. a,b. FOUNDATIONS OF BUILDINGS
39. FOUNDATIONS, ARCHAIC TREASURY (?)
40. TREASURY OF THE CITY OF ACANTHUS AND BRASIDAS

As we follow the bend to the right in the Sacred Way, the first monument situated on the left is the Athenian treasury, its entrance facing east:

The façade of the Athenian treasury (no. 21).

21. Athenian treasury

This is a marble building of the Doric order, with two columns *in antis* at the front and rich architectural sculpture including a frieze with triglyphs and metopes carved in relief, pedimental statues and acroteria, which are all exhibited in room VI in the museum and will be described later on (see p. 106-113).

The dating of the Athenian treasury is problematic. According to Pausanias (X,11,5) it was dedicated on the occasion of the Athenian victory in the battle of Marathon (490 BC). The archaeologist W. B. Dinsmoor also dates the treasury around 500-490 BC, and associates its dedication with the reformation of the Athenian Agora. He bases his argument on the increase of silver production from the mines at Laurion in 490 BC, which he believes provided the Athenian state with sufficient funds for building the walls at Piraeus as well as other public edifices. Other archaeologists suggest that

The north-western corner of the Athenian treasury, showing the remains of its roof (no. 21).

the foundations and the sculpture of the treasury should be dated in an earlier period, approximately in the last decades of the sixth century BC (530-525 BC). According to this view the dedication of this treasury could be viewed as an expression of gratitude to the Delphic oracle for assisting the expedition which resulted in the expulsion of the tyrants from Athens. Scholars supporting an earlier date for the treasury dispute the accuracy of Pausanias' testimony; they suggest that the traveller must have confused the treasury with a neighbouring monument where, according to inscriptions, the Athenians had erected the spoils of their victory at the battle of Marathon in honour of Apollo (see below no. 22).

This monument was located to the south-west of the Athenian treasury:

The south-western corner of the Athenian treasury. Triangular base of the monument dedicated by the Athenians to commemorate their victory at the battle of Marathon (no. 22).

22. Votive offering of the Athenians for the victory at the battle of Marathon
A triangular base made of limestone has been discovered at this point. According to an inscription, on this monument stood the trophies dedicated by the Athenians to Apollo from the Persian spoils gathered at the battle of Marathon.

To the north-east of the Athenian treasury are:

23. Bouleuterion (Council House or Parliament)
These are the foundations of an Archaic rectangular building made of limestone, which has been identified with the Bouleuterion of Delphi. The representatives (*prytaneis*) of the city, who were supposed to protect the state laws and institutions as well as supervise social welfare, held their meetings in this building.

Opposite the Athenian treasury and the Bouleuterion, to the right as we walk along the Sacred Way, the foundations of three buildings are preserved:

24. Treasury of Cnidus (?)
Following the description of Pausanias (X,11,5) this should be the location of the Cnidian treasury. It was an Ionic building with two columns *in antis*, to which has also been attributed a Caryatid found in the area (see p. 82, no. 5). The surviving votive inscription does not provide us with any information about the occasion of this dedication. It should most probably be dated to circa 550-544 BC, just before the occupation of Cnidus by the Persians, circa 550-540 BC.

25-26. Foundations of treasuries (?)
The foundations of no. 26 belong to a Doric building decorated on the front with a frieze of triglyphs and metopes. It may have been the treasury dedicated by the people of Syracuse after defeating the Athenians in 413 BC (Pausanias, X,11,5).
The evidence concerning the building no. 25 is much more scarce, but it has been suggested that this might be the so-called Aeolic treasury.

Returning to the left side of the Sacred Way, as we approach the temple of Apollo, behind the Bouleuterion and the retaining-wall supporting the Athenian treasury, we encounter the following monuments:

27. Sanctuary of Asclepius
Judging from the votive offerings found in this area the cult of Asclepius must have flourished in Delphi in the 4th century BC. The sanctuary of the god was built over the foundations of an Archaic treasury dated to circa 548 BC. The treasury was made of Italian stone which suggests that it may have been dedicated by the Etruscans.

28. Water spring or fountain of Asclepius

29. Sanctuary of Gaia, the goddess of Earth
To the north of the Bouleuterion (see above no. 23) was most probably the sanctuary of Gaia, who is thought to be the oldest deity worshipped in Delphi. In this sanctuary may have been located the sacred spring, which was supposed to be guarded by the dragon Python (see p. 16). Foundations of an Archaic building have also been found in the area; this may have been either a treasury, or more likely a small temple (a shrine) dedicated to the goddess.

In the area to the east of the Bouleuterion we encounter several monuments, among which are some related to the old stone cults in Delphi (see p. 17):

30. Rock of the Sibyl
It is attested that when Gaia was the dominant deity in the sanctuary of Delphi the oracles were delivered by the Sibyl, who was seated on a sacred rock. According to Plutarch (*Moralia,* 398B-E) the rock was supposed to be next to the Bouleuterion.

31. Boeotian offering
In front of the rock of the Sibyl stands the base of a Boeotian offering dated to the 4th century BC.

32. Stone of Leto
To the east of the rock of the Sibyl (no. 30) is another stone attributed to Leto. According to a variation of the myth, Apollo arrived at Delphi at a very young age accompanied by his mother, Leto. It was thought that at this location the god fought with the dragon Python, who guarded the sanctuary of Gaia.

33. Naxian sphinx
The mountain slope to the north of the stone of Leto has been built up to accommodate an Ionic column of exceptional height bearing a sphinx on its capital. This monument was dedicated by Naxos around 570-560 BC, a period of great prosperity for the island. The height of this offering was most impressive, reaching in total 12.10m. According to an honorary decree dated to 328-7 BC and inscribed on the base of the column, the privilege of *promanteia* (the right of precedence in consultation) was granted to the Naxians. As mentioned above, this was the highest honour that could be granted to those favoured by the city of Delphi. The sphinx and the column capital from the monument are exhibited in room III of the museum and will be discussed in detail later on (see p. 80-81, no. 3).

To the east of the Naxian sphinx is:

34. Athenian stoa
According to the inscription on the stylobate, the stoa was dedicated by the Athenians to accommodate the first-fruits (*akrothinia*) of the spoils from naval battles and other victories on land. The dedication of military spoils to Apollo may be interpreted as an expression of religious fervour and respect, while at the same time it was a great opportunity to demonstrate and promote the naval

Part of the votive inscription on the stylobate of the Athenian stoa (no. 34).

The façade of the Athenian stoa (no. 34).

and military power of the city in a panhellenic sanctuary, where it would have a major appeal to the entire Greek world. Thus, the dedication of the stoa and the treasury by the Athenians may be interpreted not only as expressions of respect and faith to Apollo, but also as manifestations of Athenian sovereignty. The stoa was probably initially built to house the finest spoils from the victorious naval battle at Salamis (480 BC) and was later used for the exhibition of loot from other Athenian victories as well. It was a long, narrow building with a wooden roof and seven or eight Ionic columns made of Pentelic or Parian marble on the front. It was one of the earliest buildings with an Ionic colonnade, an innovation emphasising once more the leading role of Athens. In front of the stoa are two bases of Hellenistic statues; one bore the statue of Attalus II, the king of Pergamon, dedicated by the city of Delphi at the beginning of his reign (159-138 BC).

Opposite the Athenian stoa, the area with the sacred stones and the Naxian sphinx, on the right-hand side as we head upwards along the Sacred Way, are preserved the foundations of buildings and the bases of votive offerings which cannot be securely identified. In antiquity this area was a courtyard with votive offerings, known as the Halos:

35. The Halos

The celebration of the 'Septeria' took place at the Halos every eight years. This festival involved the performance of a sacred drama re-enacting the slaughter of the dragon Python by Apollo. The event possibly signified a purification ceremony for the city as well as for the worshipped god. A staircase, called the *doloneia*, situated at the centre of the Halos, was probably used during the ceremony to provide access to the entrance of the imaginary cave, where the Python was hiding.

To the east of the doloneia are preserved the foundations of a single room:

37. Corinthian treasury

The foundations of this rectangular building may be identified with the Corinthian treasury. This was probably the earliest treasury dedicated in Delphi. It was originally a personal offering by the tyrant Cypselus (657-628 BC), which, after his death, was said to have been dedicated by the city of Corinth.

To the east of the Corinthian treasury two buildings are preserved:

38 a,b. Foundations of buildings

The building numbered 38a faces west and had two columns *in antis* at the entrance. It may be identified with the treasury of Cyrene. This dedication should be dated before 322-321 BC, when, according to the inscription written on one of the *antae*, Delphi granted to Cyrene the right of *promanteia*.
The building 38b faces south and its identity remains unknown.

On the right-hand side as we walk towards the temple are:

39. Foundations, possibly of an Archaic treasury

40. Treasury of the city of Acanthus and Brasidas

Next to no. 39 are the foundations of a treasury with two columns *in antis*. It was probably dedicated by the people of Acanthus, on the peninsula of Chalcidike, to commemorate their liberation from Athenian sovereignty in 423 BC, with the assistance of the Spartan general Brasidas.

The south-eastern corner of the temple of Apollo and the altar dedicated by the Chians (no. 46).

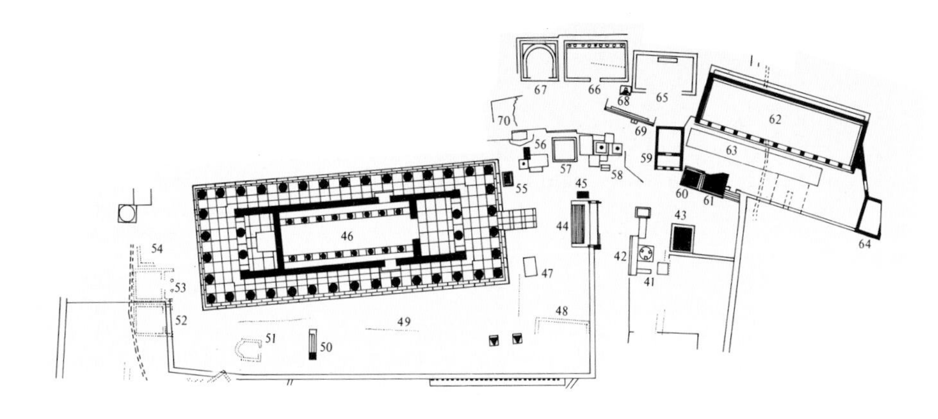

41. TRIPOD DEDICATED FROM THE SPOILS OF THE BATTLE OF PLATAEA
42. OFFERING OF TARAS
43. MONUMENT OF THE RHODIANS - A GILDED CHARIOT OF HELIOS
44. OFFERING OF THE CHIANS - ALTAR OF APOLLO
45. DEDICATION OF THE CONFEDERACY OF THE AETOLIANS - STATUE OF EUMENES II
46. THE TEMPLE OF APOLLO
47. BASE FOR THE STATUE OF AEMILIUS PAULUS
48. FOUNDATIONS OF A TEMPLE-SHAPED BUILDING
49. FOUNDATIONS
50. SPRING
51. APSIDAL BUILDING
52, 53, 54. TEMPLE-SHAPED BUILDINGS
55. ATHENIAN OFFERING - PALM-TREE AND GILT IMAGE OF ATHENA
56. OFFERING OF THE CONFEDERACY OF THE AETOLIANS - STATUE OF PRUSIAS II
57. POSSIBLY THE BASE OF THE STATUE OF APOLLO "SITALKAS"
58. OFFERINGS OF THE DEINOMENIDS - GOLDEN TRIPODS
59. FOUNDATIONS OF AN ARCHAIC TREASURY
60. BASE OF THE STATUE OF ATTALUS I
61. BASE OF THE STATUE OF EUMENES II
62. STOA OF ATTALUS I
63. PEDESTAL FOR THE OFFERINGS OF ATTALUS I
64. TEMPLE-SHAPED BUILDING
65. TEMENOS OF NEOPTOLEMUS
66. MONUMENT OF DAOCHUS
67. NICHE OF A VOTIVE OFFERING
68. POSSIBLY THE LOCATION OF THE "COLUMN OF THE DANCING GIRLS"
69. POSSIBLY PEDESTAL FOR THE OFFERINGS OF THE CORCYRANS
70. CASSOTIS SPRING (?)

Continuing our ascent along the Sacred Way we first pass through the area to the east of the entrance to Apollo's temple, where in antiquity stood rich and important votive offerings:

41. Tripod dedicated from the spoils of the battle of Plataea

Today, a circular pedestal with three steps stands here. According to the descriptions given by Herodotus and Pausanias, on this base stood a golden tripod borne on the heads of three bronze snakes; the bodies of the snakes were wrapped around one another and on the spirals formed by the assemblage were inscribed the names of the cities that participated in the battle of Plataea (479 BC). Part of the bronze column was transported to Constantinople by Constantine the Great and can be seen today in the Hippodrome Square in front of the cathedral of Hagia Sophia in Istanbul.

42. Offering of Taras

A base is partially preserved, to the west of the tripod of Plataea, which once belonged to a monument dedicated by the people of Taras. According to the votive inscription the offering was made from the spoils taken by the Tarantines from their barbarian neighbours. Pausanias (X,13,10) reports that it was the work of the sculptors Onatas from Aegina and Ageladas from Argos and included statues of riders and warriors on foot representing the kings of Taras riding against their enemies.

43. Monument of the Rhodians - a gilded chariot of Helios

To the east of the tripod of Plataea (no. 41) is an inscribed pedestal which held a gilded chariot of Helios (Sun), the patron god of the city of Rhodes. The monument cannot be securely dated; possibly it was dedicated c. 304 BC.

Having reached the end of the Sacred Way, in front of the entrance to the temple, the area to our left is dominated by the altar of Apollo:

44. Offering of the Chians - the altar of Apollo

According to the votive inscription, the altar was dedicated by the island of Chios to Apollo in the first half of the 5th century BC. The altar was approximately 9x5m in size. Inscriptions and decrees concerning Chios have been found on its side walls. One of the decrees testifies that the island had been granted the privilege of *promanteia* by Delphi.

45. Dedication of the Confederacy of the Aetolians - statue of Eumenes II

To the north of the altar is the base of the statue of the king of Pergamon, Eumenes II. It was dedicated by the Confederacy of the Aetolians and is dated between 197 and 182 BC.

46. The temple of Apollo

The foundations preserved today belong to the temple of the 4th century BC, which was built between 370 and 329 BC. It was a Doric temple made mainly of stone and partly of marble, with 6x15 columns on the peristyle. It has a pronaos (front porch) and an opisthodomos (back porch), both with two columns *in antis*, flanking the cella in the centre. The famous quotations spoken by the seven sages were inscribed on the walls of the pronaos, where the omphalos of Delphi might also have been placed. Inside the cella are the foundations of two double Ionic colonnades. The *adyton* was at the west part of the cella; there was supposed to be a chasm in the earth emitting the fumes which were thought to give the Pythia the ability to predict.

According to ancient written sources (e.g. Pausanias, X,24,4) inside the temple were several sacred points which, unfortunately, have not been located with certainty; these were: the altars of Poseidon and Hestia, the tomb of Diony-

The retaining wall supporting the temple of Apollo.

sus, statues of two of the Fates (Moirae), Zeus and Apollo and the throne the Greek poet Pindar dedicated to Apollo, where he used to sit and compose his songs to the god.
The temple had rich architectural sculpture: Apollo dominated the representation on the east pediment, while Dionysus was the protagonist on the west pediment. This selection of decorative themes is related to the history of the sanctuary, where both gods were supposed to be venerated alternatively during the year (see p. 16-17). On the metopes above the exterior colonnade (peristyle) hung gilded shields commemorating victories against barbarian enemies: the offerings on the east and north metopes were from the battle at Marathon (490 BC) and on the west and south metopes from the victory of the Aetolians against the Gauls (279 BC).
Earlier architectural phases have been detected below the foundations of the 4th century temple. The previous phase was the so-called temple of the Alcmaeonidae. It was built around the end of the 6th century BC after the completion of a retaining wall which was constructed to support it. Its plan was similar to that of the 4th century temple. Two water pipes end in the foundations of the west wing. This evidence probably confirms the testimony that the water of the Cassotis spring, which was thought to inspire Pythia's prophecies (see p. 19), passed through the cella of the Archaic temple.

The preserved columns of the temple of Apollo (no. 46).

The east pediment and the larger part of the eastern façade of the 'temple of the Alcmaeonidae' were made of marble. On the pediment Apollo was represented in a chariot, possibly at the moment of his arrival at Delphi, flanked by scenes of animal fights at the corners. A Gigantomachy was depicted on the west pediment, where a chariot was also the central axis of the scene. The acroteria were winged Nikae.
The remains of an even earlier architectural phase belong to a limestone building dated to around the middle of the 7th century BC and constructed by the architects Trophonius and Agamedes. Pausanias (X,5,9 ff), finally, mentions the ancient tradition referring to three much earlier temples: the earliest temple was made of laurel from Tempe, the middle was made by bees from their wax and feathers and the last was made of bronze.

Our tour continues in the area to the south of Apollo's temple, which is bordered by the retaining wall supporting the temple:

47. Base for the statue of Aemilius Paulus

To the south-west of the altar (see no. 44) and at the south-eastern corner of the temple is a base which once held a statue of Aemilius Paulus; he was the Roman who defeated Perseus, the king of Macedon, at the battle of Pydna in 168 BC.

48. Foundations of a temple-shaped building (oikos)

49. Foundations either of the retaining wall supporting the platform of the temple before 548 BC, or bases of votive offerings.

50. Spring
This is the lowest level of an underwater spring, which was probably dedicated to the Muses.

51. Apsidal building
The plan of this building is exceptional because it has an apse facing west. It is most probably dated to the middle of the 6th century BC, and may have been a shrine dedicated to the cult of the predecessors of Apollo in the oracle.

52, 53, 54. Temple-shaped buildings
The foundations of these three temple-shaped buildings suggest that they may have been treasuries.

Having visited the best-preserved buildings in the area to the west and the south of the temple of Apollo, we return to the east to look at the monuments located close to the north-eastern corner of the temple:

55. Athenian offering - palm-tree and gilt image of Athena
Pausanias (X,15,4) mentions that here stood a bronze palm-tree – the sacred tree of Apollo – with a gilt image of Athena on it. The monument was erected by the Athenians to commemorate the double victory, on land and sea, of Cimon against the Persians at the river Eurymedon in 465 BC.

56. Offering of the Confederacy of the Aetolians - statue of Prusias II
Here stood an equestrian statue of the king of Bithynia, Prusias II. The monument must be contemporary with no. 45.

57. Possibly the base of the statue of Apollo "Sitalkas"
Apollo "Sitalkas" was supposed to be the protector of cereals. Pausanias (X,15,2-3) was impressed by the height of this statue, which exceeded 16m. It was dedicated by the Amphictyony from the spoils taken from the Phocians in the third Sacred War, and should be therefore dated after 346 BC.

58. Offerings of the Deinomenids - golden tripods
Four fragmentary bases have been found, with holes preserved on their upper surface for supporting golden tripods. These were possibly dedicated by the tyrants of Sicily, Gelon, Hieron, Polyzalus and Thrasybulus, to commemorate their victory against the Carthaginians at the battle of Himera in 480 BC. On part of the votive inscription, preserved on one of the pedestals, we read that Gelon, the son of Deinomenes, dedicated to Apollo a golden tripod and a Nike made by Bion, the son of Diodorus of Miletus.

59. Foundations of an Archaic treasury

60. Base of the statue of Attalus I

61. Base of the statue of Eumenes II
The statues nos 60 and 61 were probably dedicated by the Amphictyony in c. 182 BC to honour the kings of Pergamon for their benefactions.

To the north of the monuments nos 60 and 61 in an area, known as the 'exedra of Attalus', the following buildings were situated:

62. Stoa of Attalus I
The stoa had eleven Doric columns on the façade. According to the votive inscription, it was dedicated in 220 BC by the king of Pergamon, Attalus I Soter

Bases for the tripods of the Deinomenids (no. 58). The pedestral of Prusia's statue (no. 56) and the east façade of Apollo's temble (no. 46).

(241-197 BC). In the Roman period the stoa was converted into a reservoir.

63. Pedestal for the offerings of Attalus I
The rectangular structure in front of the stoa possibly held other offerings of Attalus I.

64. Temple-shaped building
This is a small building in the shape of a shrine which may have been used for the worship of Dionysus, the great god of Pergamon.

As we leave the monuments on the 'exedra of Attalus' and head for the area to the west we reach:

65. Temenos of Neoptolemus
The foundations of an enclosure wall, dated at the end of the 4th century BC, have been preserved. At this location may have been the sanctuary of Neoptolemus, where annual purification ceremonies were performed. According to the myth, Neoptolemus, the son of Achilles, was killed at Delphi by Orestes because he married Hermione, the woman Orestes was also in love with.

66. Monument of Daochus
This monument was accommodated in a rectangular building and stood on a pedestal 11.50m long. On the upper surface of the pedestal are preserved holes for nine marble statues. According to the inscription on the base, it was dedicated by the Thessalian tetrarch, Daochus II. The offering must have been made in the years between 339-334 BC, when

Daochus II was serving as hieromnemon at the Delphic Amphictyony. The statues represented the predecessors and descendants of Daochus II and are exhibited in room XI in the museum (see p. 130-136, nos 1 and 2).

67. Exedra of a votive offering (This monument has not been identified)

68. Possibly the location of the 'column of the dancing girls'
Here stood a column decorated with acanthus leaves on the base, the capital and at the joints of each drum. It was crowned with a group of three female figures, possibly dancers, carrying a cauldron on their heads (the preserved parts of this monument are exhibited in room XI in the museum, see p. 132, 137, no. 3a-b). The total height of the column is estimated at approximately 10.90m and considering that it probably stood on a three-stepped base the whole monument must have been about 12.50m high. A base on which the letters PAN are inscribed has recently been associated with this offering. The three characters have been completed as Pancrates, the name of a building-contractor who worked at Delphi in the second half of the 4th century BC. Although the votive inscription is fragmentary it does mention that the monument was dedicated by the Athenians. Finally, the style of the sculpture suggests that it was made around 330 BC.

Part of the sculptural group crowning the so-called column of the dancing girls (no. 68).

69. Possibly a pedestal for the offerings of the Corcyreans
It is not certain what this rectangular base held. The original dating of the monument is not secure, but the remains suggest that it must have undergone alterations in the 4th century BC.

70. Cassotis spring (?)
According to Pausanias (X,24,7), the spring was named after a Nymph of Parnassus and emerged in the *adyton* of Apollo's temple because it was believed to inspire the prophecies of Pythia. The water was conducted to Cassotis through pipes from a spring situated higher up the mountain. The Cassotis spring was built in two levels: the outlets for the water were on the upper level inside a basin, which was accessible by steps; on the lower level was a reservoir for storing the overflow and conducting it through pipes to other springs in the *temenos*.

Base of the 'column of the dancing girls' (to the right).

The theatre.

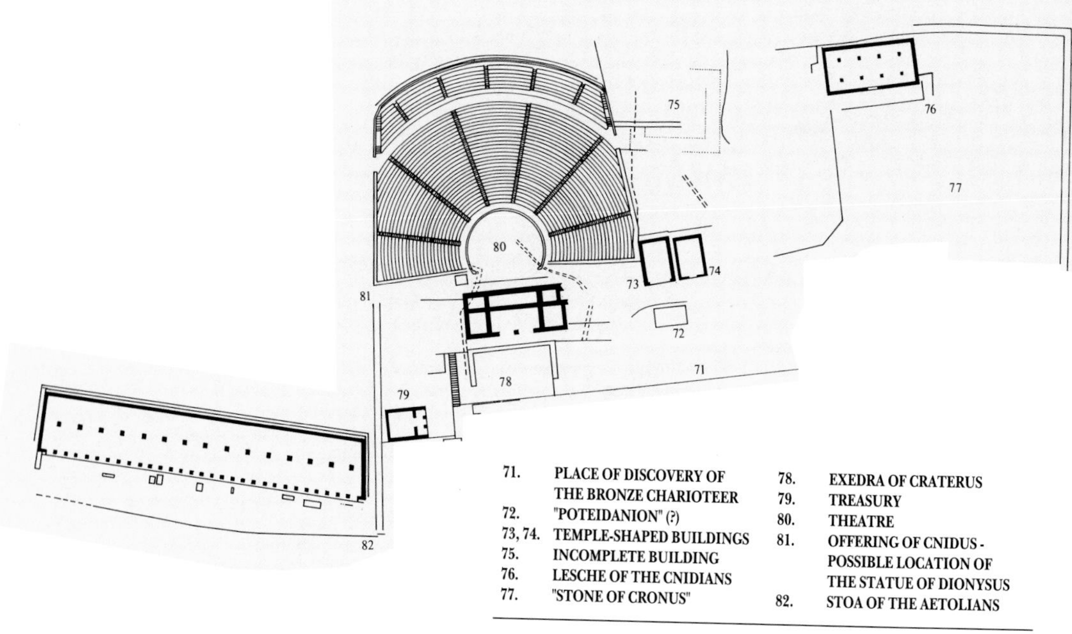

To the north of the temple of Apollo, between the temple and the theatre, was constructed a retaining wall which, according to inscriptions, was named the ischeagon. Along this retaining wall, to the west of the Cassotis spring, the bronze charioteer was found:

71. Place of the discovery of the bronze charioteer

This is a bronze statue of a young charioteer which belongs to a larger monument. Part of the base has been found with fragments of the votive inscription stating that the offering was dedicated by a tyrant of Gela to commemorate his victory in one of the chariot races at the Pythian Games. Although Pindar praises only the victory of Hieron at the Pythian Games of 470 BC, the offering may also be related to the victories of Gelon or Polyzalus in 478 or 474 BC. The parts of this monument that have been discovered are exhibited in room XII of the museum (see p. 138-143, nos 2-5).

72. 'Poteidanion' (?)

It has been attested that in the sanctuary of Apollo at Delphi there was an area dedicated to Poseidon, the so-called Poteidanion, where the god was honoured as a predecessor of Apollo in the oracle. Assuming that the 'Poteidanion' was a kind of a small sanctuary, it could be identified with the foundations of a small Archaic building found at this location. If, however, the 'Poteidanion' is identified as the altar of Poseidon inside Apollo's temple (Pausanias, X,24,4), then the use of this building remains uncertain.

To the north of the monument no. 72 are preserved:

73-74. Temple-shaped buildings (possibly treasuries)

The foundations of two buildings in the shape of small temples have been conventionally named the 'treasuries of the theatre', because they are situated at the south-eastern corner of the theatre. The architectural remains of these buildings are dated to the first half of the 5th century BC.

75. Incomplete building
The foundations of this building should be dated to the third quarter of the 4th century BC and may be associated with the upper levels of the Cassotis spring.

To the east of the incomplete building, close to the north-eastern corner of the temenos, there is a rectangular building:

76. Lesche of the Cnidians
On the retaining wall, constructed to support this building, we read inscriptions honouring the Cnidians, as well as the votive inscription stating that the Lesche was dedicated by the city of Cnidus to Apollo. It was a long, narrow building. Its interior was arranged with two colonnades of four columns each, most probably made of wood with stone bases. Pausanias (X,25,1-31,12) describes in detail the wall-paintings made by Polygnotus, one of the most important painters in antiquity. They depicted the Sack of Troy (*Ilioupersis*) and the Visit of Odysseus to the Underworld (*Nekyia*). A great number of heroes and gods were represented in both scenes. The contribution of Polygnotus to the decoration of the Lesche leads us to a date of c. 475-460 BC, although it must have also been renovated in the 4th century BC. The architectural plan and the rich decoration made the Lesche an ideal environment for gatherings, discussions and relaxation. The central space between the colonnades might have been used by athletes for exercising, if it was unroofed.

To the south of the Lesche of the Cnidians is the so-called:

77. 'Stone of Cronus'
Pausanias (X,26,6) reports that to the north of the *temenos* of Neoptolemus (no. 65) was a stone which received a daily libation of oil. At every festival they placed on it pieces of unworked wool. This stone has been identified with a rock given by Rhea to her husband, Cronus. According to the myth Cronus ate his children in order to secure his throne; Rhea, however, substituted a rock for her son Zeus. When Cronus released that he had been deceived he spat the stone from his mouth and Zeus placed it at Delphi to commemorate the event.

We return to the possible location of the so-called Poteidanion (no. 72), and looking towards the west we see:

78. Monument of Craterus
According to the inscription, preserved on two parts of limestone on the façade, the monument held a bronze group representing the lion hunt where the general Craterus saved the life of Alexander the Great. The monument was dedicated by the son of Craterus in honour of his father. The statues were made by Lysippus and Leocharis and thus should be dated around 320-300 BC.

79. Unattributed treasury

To the north of the monument of Craterus (no. 78) and in the north-western corner of the temenos is the theatre of Delphi:

80. Theatre
The present theatre, which is made of stone, is dated in the 3rd century BC.

However, this slope was most probably used as a theatre in earlier periods too, when the auditorium may have consisted of temporary rows of seats. The building of a monumental theatre with stone seats and stage was financed by Eumenes II, the king of Pergamon, in 159 BC and was improved with further alterations in the Roman period.

The theatre of Delphi follows the architectural plan of a typical ancient Greek theatre. The space arranged for the spectators is called the *cavea*; it is shaped as a semi-circle and has 35 rows of seats which can accommodate an audience of 5000 people. On the 28th row is a wide corridor (*diazoma*) dividing the *cavea* into two levels. Vertical staircases facilitate the movement of people by dividing the rows of seats into wedge-shaped sections (*kerkides*), seven on the upper level and six on the lower level of the *cavea*. The semicircular space formed at the bottom of the *cavea* is the orchestra, where during the performances the chorus stood around an altar of Dionysus. The rectangular structure in front of the *orchestra* is the stage (the *proskenion* and the *skene*), where the actors performed and the appropriate stage scenery was set up. Entrances at either side of the stage were called *parodoi*, and there were also two additional entrances at the edges of the *diazoma*.

The musical competitions for the Pythian Games took place in the Delphic theatre. The Pythian Games were first organised around 600-590 BC and originally only involved competitions in the performance of the kithara. In 586 BC the Amphictyony decided to include contests of flute-playing and singing accompanied by a flute. Athletic contests were added for the first time in 582 BC and took place in the stadium. The Pythian Games occurred every four years and the winners were awarded a laurel wreath.

Leaving the theatre from the west parodos we encounter:

81. Offering of Cnidus - possible location of the statue of Dionysus

An inscribed base has been found close to the west *parodos* of the theatre. This may belong to the statue of Dionysus which is mentioned by Pausanias (X,32,1) as an offering of the Cnidians.

To the south-west of the theatre, as we leave the temenos by one of the exits of the enclosure wall, there is an important monument:

82. Stoa of the Aetolians

This was the largest stoa in the sanctuary and was constructed in the 3rd century BC. It had twenty-nine columns on the front and inside. On the interior wall the votive inscription can be read; the monument was dedicated by the Aetolians from the spoils of their victory against the Gauls in 279 BC.

E. STADIUM

As we return to the theatre and leave through the west parodos we walk uphill towards the north-west, where we reach the Delphic stadium:

Stadium

The stadium is located to the north-west of the *temenos* of Apollo, uphill towards the mountain (approximately 30m to the north from the highest part of the *temenos*). It was built for the athletic competitions, which were introduced to the Pythian Games of 582 BC. The present structure belongs to the fourth architectural phase of the stadium, which is dated to the second half of the 2nd century AD. However, on the retaining wall to the south is preserved an inscription dated to the 5th century BC, which suggests that at least since that date athletic contests were held in the stadium. In the beginning the auditorium probably consisted of temporary row of seats. The fourth architectural phase of the stadium was financed by Herodes Atticus (103-179 AD) and provided seats made of stone from Parnassus.

The plan of the stadium is U-shaped; it has rows of seats on the north and on the south side, while the west side is a semi-circular area known as the *sphendone*. The twelve rows of stone seats preserved on the north side are divided by vertical staircases into twelve wedge-shaped sections (*kerkides*). The retaining-wall which supported the rows of seats on the south side has collapsed. The *sphendone* has six rows of seats divided into four wedge-shaped sections (*kerkides*) by three vertical staircases. On the east the grooved marble starting-slabs are still visible. The four pillars at the far end supported a triumphal arch which was the ceremonial entrance for competitors and officials. The distance between the starting and the finishing line is 177.5m in length and 28.5m in width.

The athletic contests are similar to those held in the Olympic Games, except for the omission of the four-horse chariot race and the boy's *dolichos* (a long foot-race) and the addition of the boy's *diaulos* (a double-length of the stadium foot-race). Several victories at the Pythian Games were praised by Pindar in his triumphal *Pythian Odes*, the most famous of which is the ode written for the victory of Hieron, the tyrant of Gela, in the chariot race of 470 BC.

Stadium. The four pillars at the front supported a triumphal entrance.

A VISIT TO THE MUSEUM

The first museum at Delphi was built in 1903 by the French Archaeological School in Athens and was financed by the Greek government. Until the 1960s the building was renovated on several occasions to provide more spacious rooms for as many objects as possible. The present exhibition is the result of a long project completed in the 1970s with the contribution and co-operation of many archaeologists working for the Greek Archaeological Service.
In the courtyard, in the front of the entrance to the museum, is a mosaic dated in the 5th century AD. It belonged to an Early Christian basilica and is decorated with scenes of animals, such as panthers, deer, dogs, fish, etc., and two youths holding fruit-baskets.
The rooms of the museum and their exhibits, described in the following pages, are numbered according to the attached plan. The exhibits were discovered in the excavations carried out at the archaeological site of Delphi and are mainly votive offerings, such as statues and sculpture groups, architectural remains and parts of architectural ornaments, as well as ceremonial vessels and objects for everyday use. They are made mainly of metal, marble and clay and are characteristic examples of ancient Greek art produced at the time that the oracle was at its peak; the advanced techniques developed in metal-working are demonstrated in particular by the large number of metal offerings (made of precious metals, such as gold and silver, as well as bronze). The artistic quality as well as the value of 'precious' objects not only signifies that the oracle was highly respected, but also suggests that the contributors were wealthy and powerful.

Detail from the mosaic in front of the museum (5th century AD).

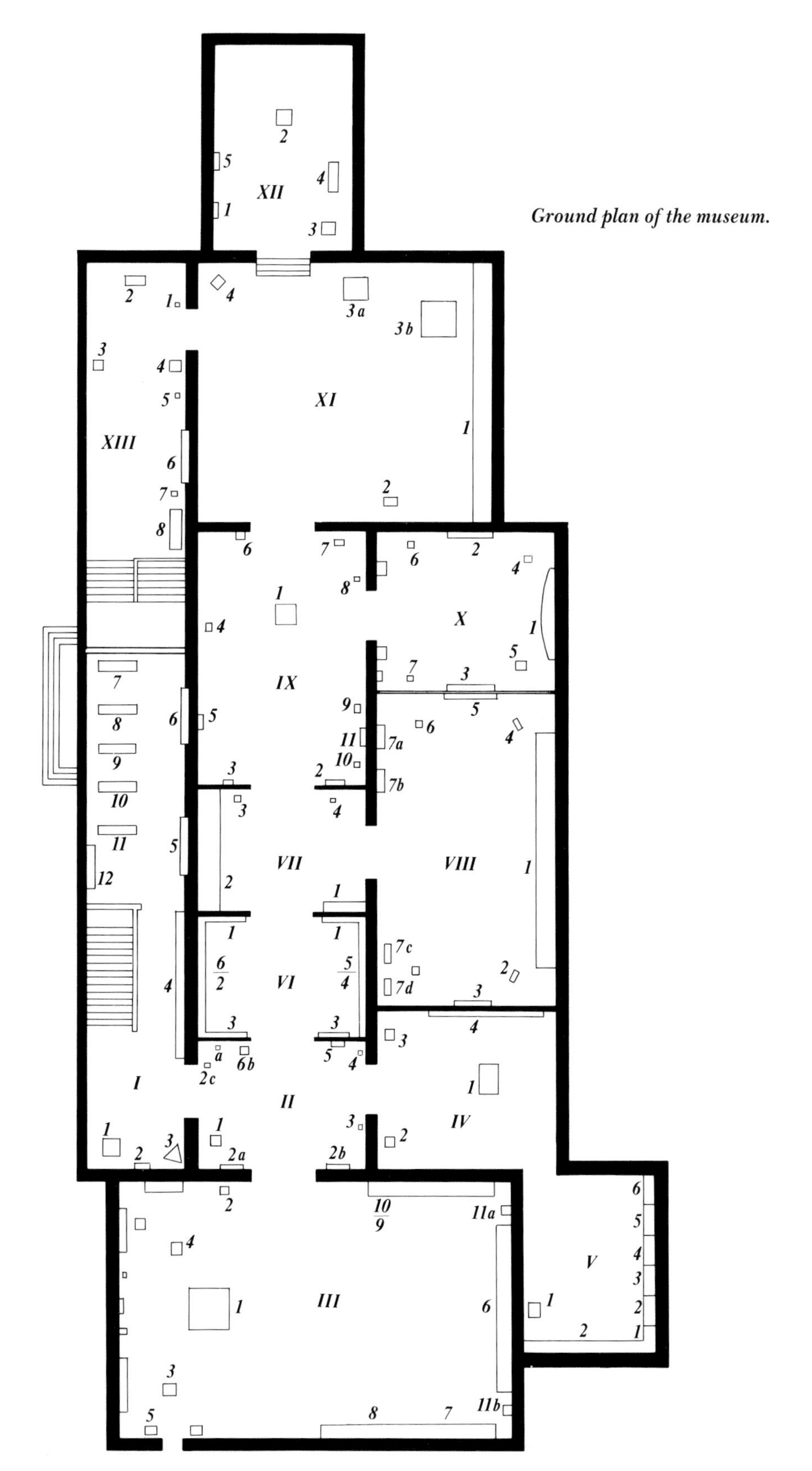

Ground plan of the museum.

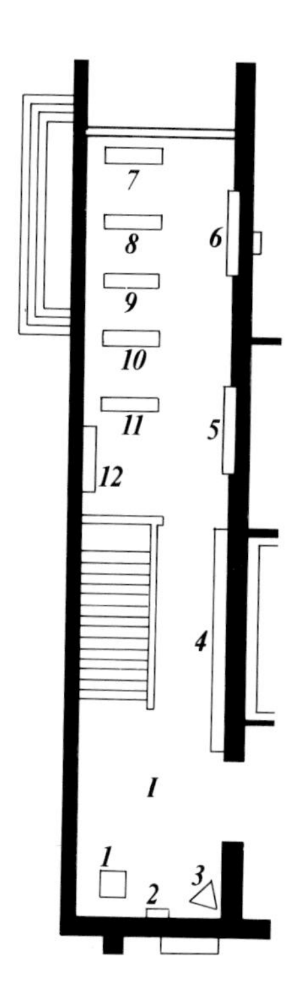

ROOM I:
'Omphalos Room'

As we go up the staircase leading to the exhibition rooms we first encounter a copy of the **omphalos of Delphi (1)**, which is Hellenistic or Roman in date. The relief decoration on its surface was possibly intended to represent the *agrenon*, a material made of woollen ribbons which covered the original omphalos inside the *adyton* of the temple of Apollo (see p. 15). The omphalos ('navel') signifies the belief that Delphi was the centre of the world; this notion originated from a myth describing Delphi as the meeting point of the two eagles sent by Zeus from opposite ends of the earth.

To the left of the omphalos is a relief crowning an **inscribed stele (2)**. On the inscription we read an honorary decree issued around 330 BC, praising Demades, an Athenian orator and politician. Represented on the relief are: on the left the goddess Athena and on the right a figure with one arm raised, who may be Apollo or a personification of the Demos (municipality) of Delphi.

Next to the relief stands a **tripod (3)** made of iron and bronze. The tripod supported a bronze cauldron dated between 750 and 650 BC. Tripods of this type were the most common votive offerings in the sanctuary of Apollo during the 8th and 7th centuries BC.

Along the wall in the narrow corridor leading to the other part of the room is a **relief frieze (4)**. It is dated to the 1st century AD and was possibly a decorative element from the stage of the Delphic theatre. The frieze is carved in relief with representations of the labours of Heracles, a popular subject in ancient Greek art from the 6th century BC (see p. 109-112). According to the myth, the panhellenic hero, Heracles, was compelled to perform a number of labours for his cousin Eurystheus, in order to purify himself of the murder of his own children. This tragic incident resulted from the madness inflicted on Heracles by the goddess Hera to revenge her husband Zeus for sleeping with Alcmene, the hero's mother. Heracles, however, carried out the assigned labours successfully and therefore, upon the completion of his tasks, he was deified and introduced to the group of the Olympian gods. The labours of Heracles depicted on the six slabs of the relief exhibited here are: the taking of the golden apples from

Copy of the omphalos of Delphi (no. 1).

Relief frieze of the 1st century AD (no. 4): a) Heracles against the Hydra of Lerna and the giant Antaios.

b) Heracles tames the horses of Diomedes and fights an Amazon.

Corinthian aryballos, 7th century BC. (show-case 6).

the Hesperidae, the abduction of Cerberus from the Underworld, followed by the confrontations with the Nemean lion, a Centaur, the Hydra of Lerna, the giant Antaios and an Amazon. There are also depicted: the abduction of the horses of Diomedes, the shooting of the Stymphalian Birds and the fight with the triple-bodied warrior, Geryon.

The following show-case **(no. 5)** contains clay vessels from Attic, Corinthian and Boeotian workshops dated from the Proto-Geometric to the Late Geometric periods (900-700 BC). Most of the vases are decorated with Geometric patterns, apart from a fragment of the Late Geometric period with a stylised representation of warriors.

The first exhibits in the next show-case **(no. 6)**, along the same wall, are objects found in a grave at Amphissa dated around 650-640 BC. These are mostly re-

Handle of a bronze cauldron, 8th century BC (show-case 7).

Sirens, cauldron-attachments, 8th century BC (show-case 8).

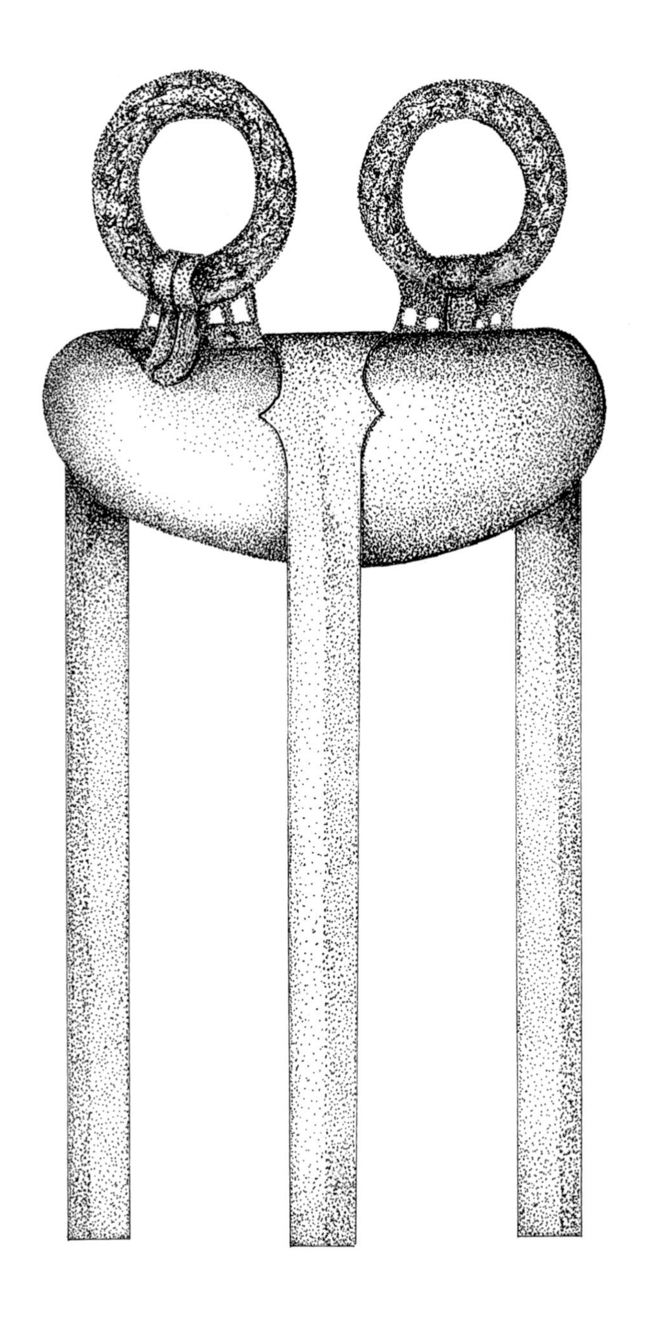

Reconstruction of a bronze cauldron with ring handles.

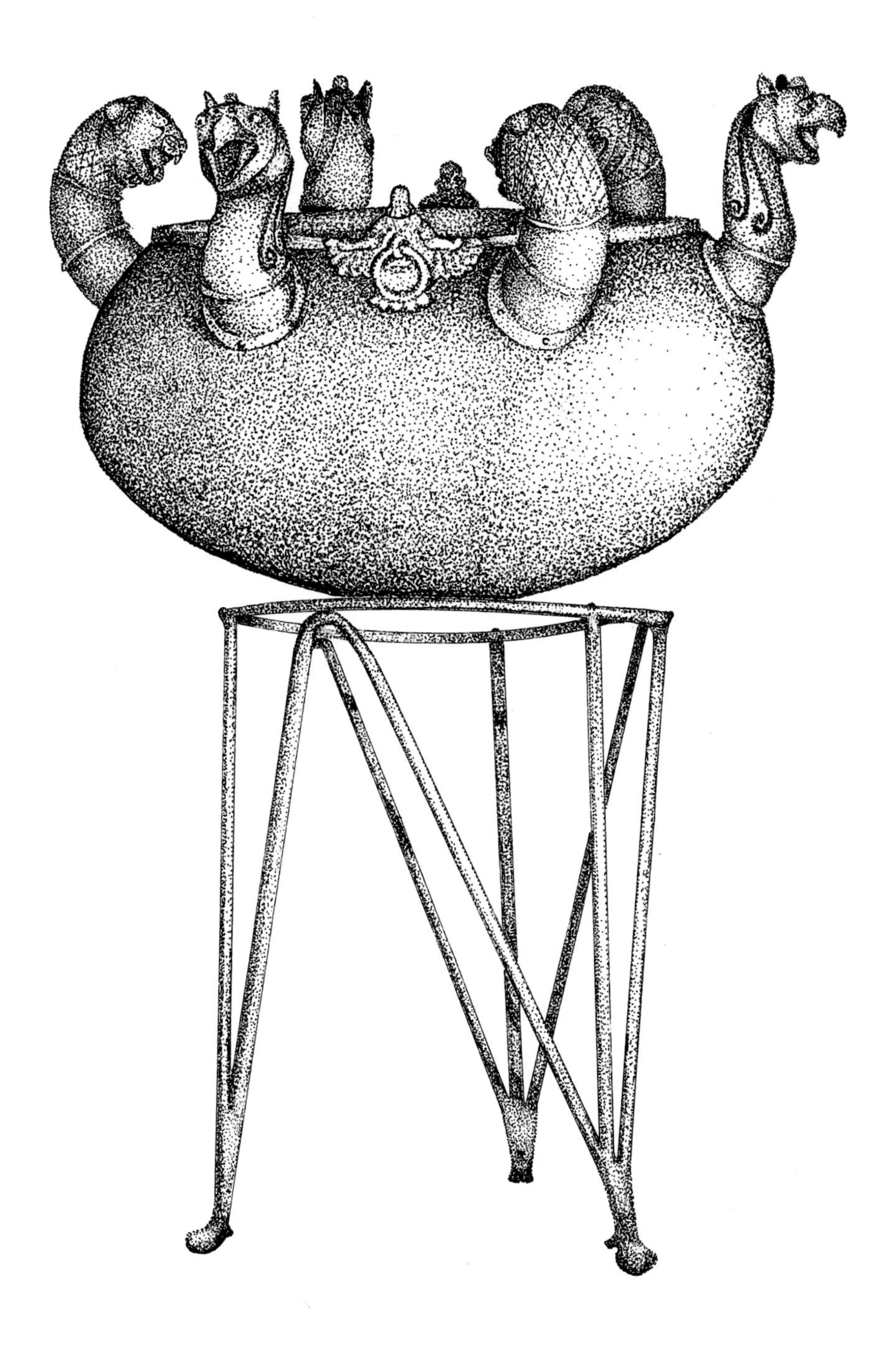

Reconstruction of a bronze cauldron and tripod. Sirens and griffins decorate the rim of the vessel.

Statuette of a naked athlete, 430-420 BC (show-case 9).

Statuette of a young man, 550-525 BC (show-case 9).

lated to the world of women: bronze fibulae and pins for fastening garments, and gold or bronze jewels such as rings and bracelets. The remaining exhibits are clay pots from Delphi: miniature aryballoi, oinochoai and a pyxis, as well as vessels of normal size, such as kantharoi, and amphorae. Characteristic are two Corinthian aryballoi, vessels used for carrying olive oil or perfumed oil, decorated with animal figures.

Fragments of bronze objects dated in the Geometric period (9th-8th centuries BC) are exhibited in show-cases 7-11. In **show-case 7** are important bronze statuettes of the 8th century BC, representing, in a schematic manner, human figures (women, warriors holding shields), horses etc.. In addition, there are other figures carved in the round used as decorative attachments placed on the rim and the handles of tripods and cauldrons. The three cauldron handles are distinctive and were attached on the vase as shown in the drawing in p. 74.

Exceptional in **show-case no. 8** is a lion's paw, which was attached to the bottom of a tripod foot. Other cauldron attachments dated to the 8th and 7th centuries BC are: heads of griffins, sirens, and bulls.

In **show-case 9** bronze male figurines are exhibited. The statuette of a naked man in action dated around 480-470 BC was probably part of a group representing Apollo's fight with Heracles for the Delphic tripod (see p. 86-87, 89-90). The bronze statuette of a ram with a human figure attached under its belly is particularly interesting; it is dated to the second or the third quarter of the 6th century BC and was an attachment for a

Bronze statuette of a ram, vase-attachment, 575-525 BC (show-case 9).

Corinthian helmet, 700-675 BC (show-case 11).

bronze vessel. The composition portrays Odysseus escaping from the cave of the Cyclops Polyphemus. Later in date is the statuette of a naked athlete pouring a libation; his stylistic characteristics and posture suggest a date close to the works of the sculptor Polycleitus, around 430-420 BC. Also impressive are: the statuette of a young man with long hair dated to 550-525 BC and possibly made by a Laconian workshop; a figurine of a naked man dated around 590-570 BC, is the product of an eastern Greek workshop (possibly Ionia or Ephesus); a bronze figurine of a greyhound which was probably a fulcrum, part of the decoration of a bed. Dated to 400-373 BC, it is the earliest extant fulcrum.

In **show-case no. 10** we see bronze vessels and parts of their ornaments, ranging in date from the 8th century BC to the Roman period.

In **show-case no. 11** the following objects are distinctive: two Corinthian helmets of the 7th century BC. Some objects from the female world: bronze bracelets with stamped decoration, fibulae and pins, as well as a mirror-cover decorated with a female head dated around 300 BC and probably made by a Corinthian workshop. Finally, notice the bronze weapons and the tools for various uses.

Objects from the Mycenean period are exhibited in the last **show-case 12)**. Most interesting are the female statuettes, which were probably supposed to portray the deities to whom they were dedicated.

Bronze mirror cover, 300 BC (show-case 11).

Right: Mycenean female figurine, 14th-13th century BC (show-case 12).

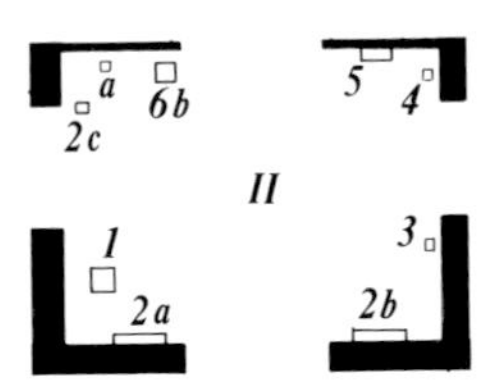

ROOM II:
'Shield Room'

To the right, as we enter the room, we encounter a **marble base (1)** which supported a marble basin. Monuments of this type are called *perirrhanteria* and were probably used for purification rituals. This one is dated to the first quarter of the 6th century BC and was made either by a Corinthian or by a Laconian workshop.

On the walls, on either side of the *perirrhanterion*, are suspended **three bronze shields (2 a-c)**. They are dated to the 7th century BC and judging from their decoration they may have originated from either Crete or Cyprus.

On the wall, on the opposite side of the entrance, are two bronze statuettes. One is a kouros-type **figurine of Apollo (3)** made by a Laconian workshop around 525 BC; he has long hair fixed with a ribbon and ringlets crowning his forehead, he wears a necklace and sandals, and his left leg is extended forward. The second statuette stands opposite no. 3 and represents a **male nude figure (4)** with the characteristic hairstyle of the so-called Daedalic statues, made by a Cretan workshop and dated to the second half of the 7th century BC.

On the left is a **bronze statuette of a cow (5)** dated to the first quarter of the 5th century BC and **two bronze heads of griffins (6 a-b)**. The latter are dated in the first half of the 7th century BC and were originally used as cauldron-attachments; one was made of hammered bronze sheets (6a) and the other was cast (6 b).

Bronze head of a griffin, 700-650 BC (no. 6b).

Bronze statuette, possibly representing Apollo, 525 BC (no. 3).

Statuette of Daedalic style, 650-600 BC (no. 4).

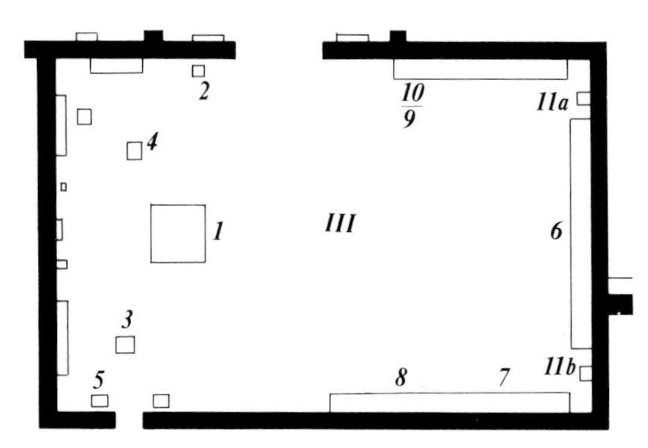

ROOM III
'Siphnian Treasury Room'

The **Naxian sphinx (1)** is singled out on the right of the entrance. This was a dedication of monumental size, originally erected to the west of the Athenian stoa (see p. 45-47, no. 34). The marble sphinx, 2.32m in height, and part of the Ionic column supporting it are exhibited here. The sphinx has the body and legs of a lion, the feathers of a bird and the head of a woman. The decorative details, mainly the breast and the feathers, are rendered in colour and incision. The sphinx was a very popular animal in Archaic vase-painting and sculpture. In antiquity it was considered to be a demonic creature with the ability to ward off evil powers, a theory which is confirmed by the extensive use of the sphinx to crown grave monuments.

The **Aeolic column capital (2)** that we see on the right as we enter room III, is dated around 530-510 BC and probably belongs to the treasury of the people of Massalia (see p. 25, no. 7 in the sanctuary of Athena Pronaia).

The remaining exhibits in this room belong to the architectural sculpture of the treasury of Siphnos (see p. 38-39, no. 14). The treasury was made entirely of marble, apart from the foundations. On the west the entablature was supported by Caryatids, parts of which (3 and 4) are exhibited on either side of the Naxian sphinx. The replacement of columns by Caryatids is an innovation introduced for the first time in the Archaic period at Delphi.

The **head of the Caryatid (3)** to the left of the Naxian sphinx belongs to the Siphnian treasury. The cavities in her hair are holes for metal ornaments. The cylindrical part above her head was carved in relief with a Dionysiac scene. The capital carried on her head is exhibited next to her, on the *echinos* is decorated with a scene of two lions attacking a deer.

On the right of the Naxian sphinx is the **head of another Caryatid (4)**. It is dated to circa 530 BC, but we cannot be certain on which building it stood. On the relief of the cylindrical part above her head Apollo and Hermes

The head of the Caryatid from the Siphnian treasury (no. 3).

Right: The Naxian sphinx, 560 BC (no. 1).

Head of a Caryatid, 530 BC (no. 4).

Caryatid from the Cnidian treasury (no. 5).

are depicted in the company of Muses and Graces.

The **torso of a Caryatid (5)**, behind and to the left of the Caryatid from the Siphnian treasury (see above no. 3), probably belongs to the treasury of Cnidus (see p. 44, no. 24). The stylistic characteristics of this statue suggest its attribution to an eastern Greek workshop of the 6th century BC.

A marble Ionic frieze decorated with representations in low relief encircled the treasury. Inscriptions as well as attributes allow us to recognise the subjects and the figures that are represented. In antiquity, details were rendered in colours and additional metal objects; the latter were affixed in holes still visible on the surface of the relief.

The **north frieze (6)**, which faced the Sacred Way, was decorated with a

Right: Detail from the north frieze of the Siphnian treasury (no. 6). The lions drawing Cybele's chariot attack a giant.

Gigantomachy. This was the battle between the Olympian gods and the children of Earth (the goddess Gaia), which started when Zeus threw their brothers, the Titans, into Tartarus (a dark place buried deep in the ground). The divine victory was accomplished with the assistance of Heracles, when Zeus prevented Gaia from supplying the giants with the magical philtre that would have saved them. The myth of the Gigantomachy describes the conflict between two major powers: the Olympian gods, representing the natural order and balance, and the giants, savage beasts living in a community without laws. The victory of the divine in the Gigantomachy signifies the establishment of the cult of the Olympian deities and their superiority, as well as the triumph of civilisation over cruelty and anarchy. The Gigantomachy is often depicted in ancient Greek art with the repetitive motif of one divine figure against one or more armed giants.
The figures on the north frieze of the Siphnian treasury are identified, from left to right, as follows: first is Hephaistus with two bags possibly to be used as bellows. Two female figures follow, who may be Demeter and her daughter Persephone fighting with two giants. The next figure, who wears an animal skin and holds a spear, may be either

Detail from the north frieze of the Siphnian treasury (no. 6). Apollo and Artemis against three giants.

Detail from the east frieze of the Siphnian treasury (no. 9). Glaucus, Aineias and Memnon.

Detail from the north frieze of the Siphnian treasury (no. 6). Ares and Hermes fight with two giants each.

The east pediment of the Siphnian treasury (no. 10). Fight of Apollo and Heracles over the Delphic tripod.

Heracles or Dionysus. In front of him stands a deity in a chariot drawn by two lions; the goddess may be Cybele as lions are usually associated with her. The divine couple shooting with their bows must be identified as Apollo and Artemis fighting with four giants, two of which are named Cantharus and Hypertas, while another named Ephialtas falls on the ground. It is worth noticing that on the shield held by one of these four giants a fragmentary inscription can be read: 'these and those that are behind'. The inscription refers to the sculptor who worked on the decoration of the treasury, and although it does not preserve his name, it does inform us that the west frieze, on the façade of the building, and the east frieze, on the back, were carved by the same sculptor.

The fragmentary chariot that follows probably belongs to Zeus because in front of it stands his wife, Hera, who raises her spear against a giant fallen on the ground. Next to Hera are: Athena fighting with the giants Berectas and Laertas, Ares who is fully armed and attacks the giants Biatas and Enaphas, while the giant Astartas lies dead on the ground, and Hermes against two giants.

The last part of the north frieze is fragmentary, but may have depicted Poseidon probably accompanied by his wife Amphitrite.

The west frieze (7) is fragmentary. The relief decoration has been interpreted as the **Judgement of Paris**, the beauty contest between Athena, Aphrodite and Hera, of which Paris of Troy was invited to be the judge. It is well known that

*Detail from the west frieze of the Siphnian treasury (no. 7).
Aphrodite dismounts from her chariot.*

Detail from the south frieze of the Siphnian treasury (no. 8). A chariot approaches an altar.

Paris selected Aphrodite because she had promised him the most beautiful woman in the world; this was the famous Helen of Troy, the wife of Menelaus, whose abduction by Paris was the alleged cause of the Trojan War.
On the frieze are represented, from left to right: Hermes leading the goddesses, Athena mounting a chariot followed by a man and a woman dismounting from a chariot; the gesture of the woman, who is fixing her necklace identifies her as Aphrodite. On the lost part of the frieze a third chariot was most probably depicted carrying Hera, and finally, Paris greeting the three deities as they arrive.
The **south frieze (8)** is very badly preserved. On the slabs exhibited here we see two men carrying a woman to a chariot, an altar, a second chariot and riders. The scene probably depicted the abduction of a woman and may be interpreted either as the abduction of Hippodameia by Pelops or as the capture of the daughters of Leucippus by the Dioscouroi. The second chariot and the riders completing the scene are suitable for both interpretations. In the first case, the event takes place during the chariot race organised by Hippodameia's father, Oinomaos, who had announced that he would honour the winner by making him his son-in-law. In the second case, the Dioscouroi, by using one chariot each, abducted the daughters of Leucippus who were playing in the sanctuary of Aphrodite.
The **east frieze (9)** portrays a **divine assembly and a duel from the Trojan War**. The inscriptions, although in some parts only fragmentary, help to identify the figures. The central figure, which is thought to represent Zeus seated on a throne, is flanked by two groups of deities. On the left are seated: Ares, a goddess, who could be either Aphrodite, or Leto, or Artemis, and Apollo. On the right are seated: Athena, Hera and Demeter. The duel scene is focused on the two adversaries and on the body of a dead warrior, fallen on the ground between them. The opponents are: Achilles on the left and Memnon on the right, supported by Automedon and Aineias respectively. According to an episode of the Trojan War mentioned in the epic *Aithiopis*, the two heroes fought over the body of Antilochus, who had been killed in a duel with Memnon. Next to the figure standing in front of the chariot, at the right end of the frieze, the name of Nestor, the elderly father of Antilochus is inscribed. On the left, behind the Trojan warriors, a chariot is depicted accompanied by Glaucus. It is very likely that the deities were not randomly divided into two groups, but according to whose side they were on at the Trojan War: on the left are the gods protecting the Trojans and on the right are the gods supporting the Achaeans. At the centre, Zeus was probably flanked by Thetis and Io, the mothers of Achilles and Memnon respectively, who probably approached him as supplicants for the lives of their sons.
The pedimental sculpture of the treasury is exceptional, because its lower part is rendered in relief instead of being totally carved in the round. The statues of the **east pediment (10)** are exhibited above the east frieze. They are in relatively good condition and depict the **fight of Heracles and Apollo over the Delphic tripod**. According to

Detail from the east frieze of the Siphnian treasury (no. 9). Divine assembly: Ares, Aphrodite or Leto or Artemis, Apollo and Zeus.

the myth, Heracles arrived at Delphi to request an oracle regarding his freedom from the fury that tortured him. The Pythia, however, refused to help him because he had killed Iphitus, the son of Eurytus and brother of Iole, to avenge Eurytus for refusing to give him Iole as his bride. In his fury Heracles took the Delphic tripod in order to found his own oracle at Pheneos. Apollo followed him and fought with him. The conflict ended only after the intervention of Zeus who threw his thunderbolt between the opponents. On the east pediment of the treasury Zeus is placed at the centre, attempting to reconcile the adversaries with the assistance of a goddess, who may be Artemis. The central group is flanked by a chariot with two horses, while at the corners are reclining figures facing towards the centre.

The sculptures of the west pediment are very badly preserved and therefore their subject has not been identified with certainty. Finally, the **acroteria** **(11 a-b)** were winged female figures who have been interpreted as Nikae (Victories).

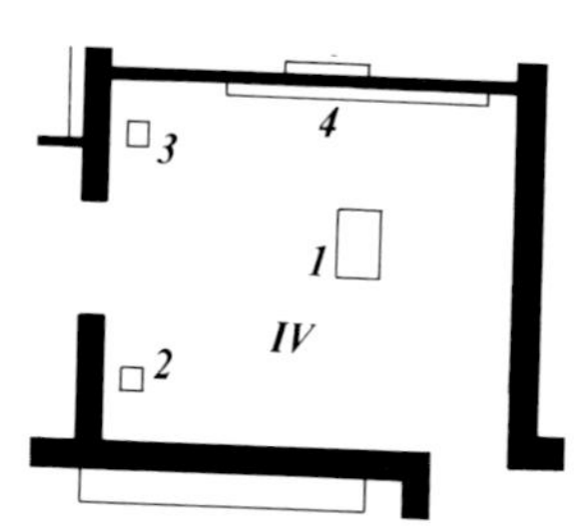

ROOM IV:
'Kouros Room'

The centre of the room is dominated by two impressive marble statues of Archaic kouroi (1), which are dated between 610-580 BC. They stand on two separate plinths, which were placed on a single inscribed base. The monument was made by the sculptor Polymedes, whose name is mentioned in the votive inscription. Unfortunately, the names of the statues have not been fully preserved in the inscription. Some scholars read the word *Anakes*, a title attributed to the Dioscouroi, and thus conclude that they were statues of the twin sons of Zeus. Others believe the kouroi represent Cleobis and Biton. Herodotus (I,31) recounts the story of Cleobis and Biton who carried their mother in her chariot to the sanctuary of Hera at Argos. As a result their mother asked Hera to reward them for their bravery and the goddess granted them a peaceful death during their sleep. It is said that the Argives sent the statues of these two heroes to Delphi, but the date of this incident is not reported. Therefore, the existing evidence does not permit the secure identification of these statues.

On either side of the entrance are two kouroi made of Parian marble. They were products of workshops based on the islands and are dated at the end of the 6th century BC. Both statues are

Details from the heads of the Archaic kouroi (no. 1).

Right: Marble statues of Archaic kouroi, decicated by the Argives (no. 1).

fragmentary: the torso and the legs are preserved from the statue on the left **(2)**, and the torso from the statue on the right **(3)**.

On the left of the central statues, along the wall, hang **five metopes made of poros (4)**. They were part of the architectural decoration of the so-called *monopteros*, the Doric building found below the foundations of the treasury of Sicyon (see p. 38, no. 13). The use of colour and incision for details can be detected on the metopes. The representations, from left to right, are as follows:

a) Argo, the boat of the Argonauts. In the background are two male figures holding a lyre; an inscription names one of them as Orpheus, the famous ancient musician who was supposed to have calmed the sea with the sound of his songs and thus ensured that the Argonauts would have a safe journey to Colchis. The scene is flanked by two horsemen, who may be identified as the Dioscouroi,

b) A female figure riding a bull. She is Europa who enchanted Zeus with her beauty. The myth says that the god transformed himself into a bull and carried Europa to Crete to seduce her,

c) The names of three figures with spears are inscribed: Castor, Polydeuces, and Idas. The animals marching between them recall the myth about the capture of cattle by the Dioscouroi and the Apharetides. Although the escapade was carried out successfully, a disagreement about the sharing of the plunder resulted in a deadly conflict be-

Kouros, end of 6th century BC (no. 2).

Fragmentary metope from the monopteros. Musicians on the Argo (no. 4a).

tween them. The missing figure must be Lynceus, Ida's brother.

d) The fourth metope depicts a scene from the Calydonian Boar Hunt. This event involved the slaying of a ferocious animal that Artemis had sent to the citizens of Calydon as a punishment, for neglecting to dedicate to her the first-fruits from their harvest. In addition to Meleager, who was the son of the king of Calydon, a large number of well-known Greek heroes participated in this hunt, such as the Dioscouroi and the Apharetides mentioned above,

Metope from the monopteros. Europa on the bull (no. 4b).

Metope from the monopteros. The Calydonian boar (no. 4d).

Metope from the monopteros. Dioscouroi and Apharetides (no. 4c).

e) On the last metope is depicted a ram, on which traces of the figure of a young boy have been preserved. The figure is identified as Phrixos as he attempts to flee from Boeotia with the assistance of his mother Nephele, to escape the hatred of his step-mother. Phrixos ended his journey at Colchis, where he sacrificed the ram that saved his life to Zeus; later he gave the Golden Fleece to his wife, the daughter of the king of Colchis. The subjects of the fifth and the first metope derive from related mythological episodes: the aim of the expedition of the Argonauts was to acquire the Golden Fleece for Jason, because Pelias, the king of Iolcus, had agreed to hand over his throne to Jason, provided that the latter would fetch him the Golden Fleece.

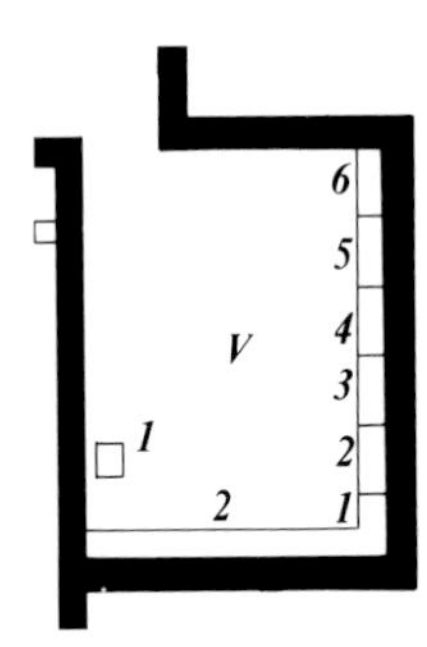

ROOM V:
'Bull Room'

The exhibits in this room are not only significant but also extremely valuable. They are dated from the 8th to the 5th century BC and are made mainly of iron, precious metals and ivory as well as of clay, wood and glass. They were stored in two deposits, which were brought to light in 1939 by excavations carried out at the area of the Halos, to the south of the Athenian stoa (see p.47, no. 35). The construction of such deposits may have been dictated by various reasons, such as the threat of a hostile invasion, or the need to store valuable objects after the destruction of a building through the atrocities of war or by disastrous weather conditions.

The archaeological finds date both deposits around the middle of the 5th century BC. It has been suggested that the objects stored in these deposits were the offerings of Croesus, the king of Lydia, which according to Herodotus (II,50) were priceless. The existing evidence, however, is not sufficient to confirm this theory.

There are two distinctive objects in room V, these are: a bronze incense-burner supported by a peplos kore (1) and a silver bull (2). **The bronze incense-burner (1)** is only 16cm high and is dated to 460-450 BC. It consists of a woman dressed in a peplos who has her arms raised to support a cauldron, which was most probably used for

Bronze incense-burner, 460-450 BC (no. 1).

Right: Silver statue of bull, 600-550 BC (no. 2).

burning aromatic herbs and plants. Notice how the weight carried by the figure is not reflected at all in her body. She stands upright and only the slight turn of her head to the right might allude to the weight she carries.

The **silver bull (2)** is a rare sample of hammered work of almost life size. Although, the hammering technique was extensively used in Archaic Greece, only small bronze statues have been found, and there is none in silver as a parallel to this bull. The statue was constructed with a wooden core on which the silver sheets were hammered. These metal sheets were fixed on a frame made of silver-plated bronze rods which were joined with rows of silver nails. Some parts of the bull, such as the eyes, the horns, the lower part of the neck and the genitals were gilded. The technical and stylistic characteristics of this work suggest it originated from Ionia and date it to the first half of the 6th century BC.

The remaining objects are placed in show-cases which are numbered from right to left, as we face the next wall. The most impressive exhibits in **show-cases nos 1** and **2** are the ivory plaques decorated in relief with figures step-

Ivory relief plaque. Departure of a warrior and detail (show-case 1).

Right: Ivory relief plaque. Phineus - Harpies and Sons of Boreas (show-case 2).

ping on a single base. They are dated to circa 570 BC and were possibly made by a Corinthian workshop. They were probably part of the decoration of either a wooden box or the throne of the chryselephantine statue of Apollo (see below show-case 3). On one of the plaques in **show-case 1** is depicted the departure of a warrior in a chariot, in the presence of four armed figures. Another relief in **show-case 2** is also important, it represents two Harpies running away with the food of Phineus, the king of Thrace, while they are pursued by the sons of Boreas. If we look carefully we notice an interesting detail on the table to the right, where part of Phineus' hand has been preserved. According to the myth, Zeus punished Phineus with blindness and sent the Harpies to torture him by stealing his food. Phineus was condemned because he blinded his sons, who were deceitfully accused by his second wife, their stepmother, of ill-treating her. Phineus was freed from his torment by the sons of Boreas, Calaes and Zetes, who passed through Thrace during their journey to Colchis with the Argonauts (see p. 94-97). Phineus won his freedom from the Harpies by advising the Argonauts on the safest route leading to Colchis and by sending favourable winds for their journey.

The most prominent exhibits in the **central show-cases (nos 3 and 4)** are three ivory heads. They are probably parts of chryselephantine statues. The technique for constructing chryselephantine statues was already developed in the Archaic and Classical periods, when it was magnificently used for two cult statues made by the sculptor Pheidias, the statue of the goddess Athena in the Parthenon and the statue of Zeus at Olympia. The torso of the statues was wooden and decorated with golden sheets, while the head and other exposed parts of the body, such as the feet and the arms, were made of ivory. It has been suggested that the three heads exhibited here were parts of a sculptural group representing the Delian Triad (Apollo, Artemis and their mother Leto).

Two of the heads, which are not in good condition, are exhibited in **show-case no. 3**. Their small size suggests that they might belong to female statues. One has been reconstructed wearing a golden crown (diadem) and has been identified as Artemis, while the other, which is very badly destroyed, is thought to represent Leto. Other parts of these statues have also been found, such as arms, fingers and feet, but it is not certain to which of the statues they belonged.

The head in **show-case no. 4** is in much better condition. It is larger than natural size and possibly depicts Apollo himself. The holes on its surface were intended for the inlaid eyes and eyebrows. We know that in antiquity the eyes of the statue were made of bone

Golden plaque from the chryselephantine statue of Artemis (show-case 4).

Left: Head from the chryselephantine statue of Artemis (show-case 3).

a.

c.

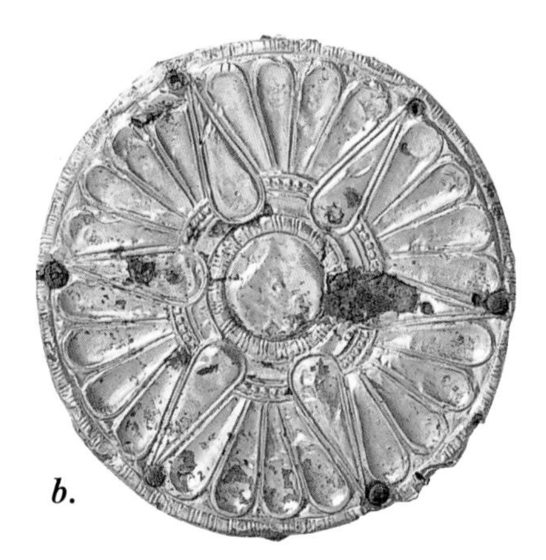

b.

Golden plaques from the decoration of chryselephantine statues
a. Medusa
b. Anthemium
c. Griffin (show-case 4).

and the ears were worked separately before being attached to the head. The head-dress was attached to the upper surface of the head and was formed by sheets of gilded silver. Two plaques hammered in gold can be dated to the middle of the 6th century BC. Their large size and shape suggest that they were probably placed on the garment worn over the legs of the figure. Each plaque is divided into two vertical columns decorated with real or imaginative animals. The subject matter of these plaques suggests that it would be more suitable to attribute them to the statue of Artemis, the goddess of hunting, than to the statue of Apollo.

Other decorative parts from the chryselephantine statues exhibited in show-case no. 4 are: a necklace with beads in the shape of a lion muzzle, gold rosettes, gilded sheets hammered with animal figures, and gold plaques with relief decoration: one square with a griffin and two semi-circular with a Medusa; the gold double anthemium was probably part of the decoration of a throne. Finally, the gold phiale in show-case no. 4 was probably held by the statue of Apollo.

A male statuette made of ivory and bone **in show-case no. 5** is remarkable. The figure holds a spear in his right hand, while with the left hand he strokes a wild animal, a lion or a panther. The intimacy between the man and the beast signifies the divine identity of the former. The technique and the stylistic characteristics of this statue suggest its eastern origin and date it to the first half of the 7th century BC. The reverse of this statue is left unfinished, which suggests that it was attached somewhere, perhaps on the surface of a wooden box.

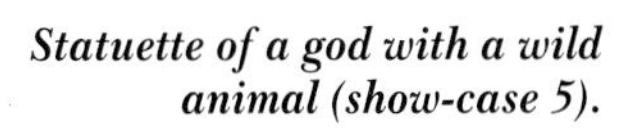

Statuette of a god with a wild animal (show-case 5).

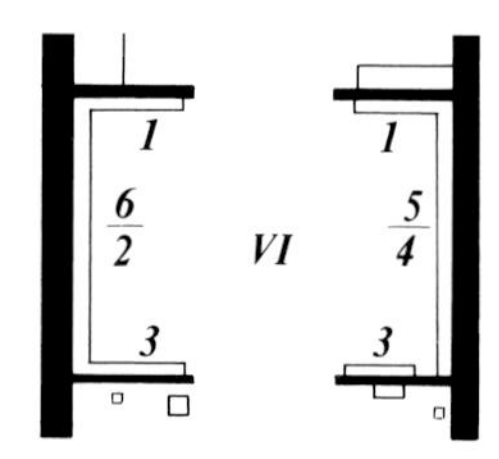

ROOM VI:
'Athenian Treasury Room'
(see p. 42-43, no. 21)

This is a marble building of the Doric order with two columns in *antis* on the façade. It was decorated with metopes, pedimental sculpture and acroteria. The style of the statues and comparisons with similar compositions in vase-painting suggest that the architectural sculpture could be dated to c. 500 BC.

The metopes encircle the building, six on the ends and nine on the sides. It is the first complete group of metopes, a unique find from Mainland Greece in the Archaic period. They were carved with mythological representations, probably by five Athenian sculptors.

On the wall opposite the entrance of room 5, **the south metopes (1)** are exhibited. This group of metopes, which represents the labours of Theseus, would be the first to be seen by the pilgrims walking along the Sacred Way. Looking at the south metopes, from left to right, we recognise the hero fighting the following opponents: a) the Minotaur, the Cretan creature with the body of a man and the head of a bull. The Athenians were obliged to send seven youths and seven maidens every nine years to be given as prey to the Minotaur. This horrible tribute was paid to the king of Crete, Minos, towards the purification of the city for the death of his son in Athens, b) an Amazon, c) the bull destroying Marathon, d) on the fourth metope the representation of Theseus with the goddess Athena interrupts the fighting episodes. On the last two metopes the hero is shown against: e) Cercyon at Eleusis, the brigand who enforced passers-by to wrestle with him before killing them, and f) Skiron, at the Cliffs of Skiron (now known as Kakia Scala), who compelled travellers to wash his legs and then threw them to the sea. The episodes on the last two metopes took place during the journey of Theseus from Troizen -the country of his mother, Aithra- to Athens, where his mortal father, Aigeus, was king. The events on the first three metopes, however, were supposed to have occurred after Theseus had arrived in Athens. Therefore, the fourth metope was probably supposed to connect these two groups representing the different cycles in the hero's life. The labours of Theseus on his journey from Troizen signify his passage from childhood to manhood when he became the capable successor of his father to the throne of Athens. This theory is confirmed by the composition on the fourth metope, where the city-patron, the goddess Athena herself, welcomes the future king of the city.

On the left we see the **east metopes (2)**, on which an Amazonomachy is depicted. The composition is arranged in groups of two. It is not clear which Amazonomachy is presented here, because the Amazons, who were a self-suf-

Theseus and an Amazon. From the south metopes of the Athenian treasury (no. 1).

Ὁ Θησεὺς καὶ ἡ Ἀμαζὼν Ἀντιόπη.
Thésée et Antiope, reine des Amazones.

Theseus and Athena. From the south metopes of the Athenian treasury (no. 1).

ficient community of female warriors, were supposed to be strong and dangerous opponents of both Heracles and Theseus.ur

As we turn towards the entrance wall, we face the **north metopes (3)**, which are not well-preserved. The iconographic theme is the labours of Heracles (see p. 70-73). On the first and the last metopes, as we look at them from left to right, are preserved only traces of the figure of a warrior. On the remaining metopes the following adversaries of Heracles have been identified: b) the Nemean lion, c) the Ceryneian hind, d) a warrior with a shield, who may be Cycnus, the son of the god Ares, who lay in ambush on the road to the Delphic oracle, to rob and kill the pilgrims going to the sanctuary, and e) a Centaur.

Finally, on the left are the **west metopes (4)**, on which one episode from the deeds labours of Heracles is

Theseus and the Marathon bull. From the south metopes of the Athenian treasury (no. 1).

Theseus and Skiron. From the south metopes of the Athenian treasury (no. 1).

unfolded: the fight with Geryon and the stealing of his cattle. Geryon was supposed to be a creature with three bodies and three heads; he owned cattle which were guarded by Eurytion, the son of Ares, and Orthrus, a dog with two heads and the tail of a snake. The cattle are shown on most of the metopes; on the fourth metope Heracles is standing next to Orthrus who is lying dead on the ground, and on the fifth is Geryon. It should be noted that the progressive depiction of a mythological episode in a series of metopes, ignoring the intermediary triglyphs of the Doric frieze, is very rare in ancient Greek art.

The pedimental compositions are fragmentary and are exhibited above the east and the west metopes respectively. Fragments from statues of warriors carved in the round have been found. The study of the position of the figures on the plinths preserved on the horizontal surface of the **west pediment** suggests that an episode of the Trojan War was depicted, with Heracles and Telamon as the protagonists. A female head has been attributed to the **east pediment**, possibly representing Athena. The goddess may have been in a frontal posture as the central axis of the scene. According to some scholars, the meeting of Theseus with his friend Peirithous before going to the Underworld was depicted on this pediment. The acroteria were Amazons on horses, which gave the impression that they

Heracles and the Nemean lion. From the north metopes of the Athenian treasury (no. 3).

were ascending towards the crest of the pediment.

It is worth commenting on the selection of the subjects for the decoration of the Athenian treasury. The chosen myths honour mainly two heroes, Theseus and Heracles, whose labours are depicted in single panels with the repetitive representation of the protagonist. On the one hand is Heracles, the son of Zeus and Alcmene, who fought dangerous opponents thanks to his physical strength and bravery and was rewarded, at the end of his life, with a position among the gods at Olympus. On the other hand is Theseus, the son of Aithra, who had both divine and mortal fathers, Poseidon and Aigeus respectively. Theseus was the glorious Athenian king who unified the Attic demes under a centralised government, and also risked his life on various occasions to protect his city. It has been argued that in Athens the achievements of those two heroes were used as a means of political propaganda. Heracles was popular in the Attic art of the second half of the 6th century BC, the era of the tyrant Peisistratus, when, according to the theory of the well-known archaeologist J. Boardman, Heracles' figure in art was supposed to personify the state as well as the tyrant himself. Towards the end of the 6th and the beginning of the 5th century BC the representations of myths involving Theseus increased in number and in addition, the hero's bones were transported by Cimon from Skyros to Athens; both incidents may be associated with the belief that Theseus represented 'democratic ideals'. This theory is confirmed by the arrangements of the metopes on the treasury; although both heroes are honoured, Theseus seems to be the more privileged since the south metopes were seen first by the visitor approaching the building from the Sacred Way.

Heracles and the Ceryneian hind stag. From the north metopes of the Athenian treasury (no. 3).

Right: Heracles and Cycnus. From the north metopes of the Athenian treasury (no. 3).

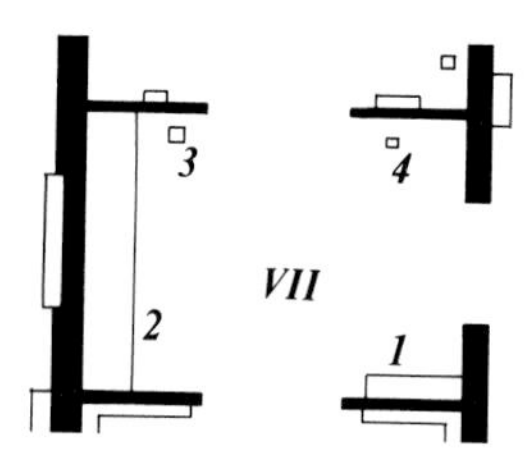

ROOM VII:
'Hymn to Apollo Room'

On the walls of the Athenian treasury were **inscribed hymns in honour of Apollo (1)**. These are exhibited on the right-hand side as we enter room VII from room VI. The hymns may have been written by a member of an actor's group and were probably recited at the Pythaid. The Pythaid was a festival organised by the Athenians in the 2nd century BC and involved a procession from Athens to Delphi which was completed with the offering of a sacrifice at the altar of Apollo and the performance of various contests. The hymns praise Apollo, Delphi and Parnassus, and appeal to the Muses to descend from the mountains of Helicon and Parnassus and sing in honour of Phoebus. On some inscriptions the musical annotation for the musical instruments accompanying the songs have also been carved together with the lyrics. This is a very important discovery for the history of music and has contributed enormously to experiments reviving ancient music.

On the wall, to the left of the entrance, is exhibited the **west pediment (2)** of the temple of Apollo which was completed around 505 BC. The construction of this temple was financed by the Athenian family of the Alcmaeonidae, who had been exiled by the tyrant Peisistratus and intended to gain favour and support to prepare their return to Athens. The amount of money they supplied for this purpose was sufficient to allow the use of marble for the east façade, while the rest of the temple was made of limestone. The theme of the west pediment is a Gigantomachy (for the myth see p. 82-85). A figure striding to the right and dressed in chiton and himation with an aegis is identified as Athena; she fights a giant collapsing to the ground. A fragmentary male torso and parts of two horses have also been attributed to this pediment.

To the right of the pediment is a **marble kouros-type statue of a draped man (3)** dated to the beginning of the 5th century BC. Opposite no. 3 is the **statue of a peplos kore (4)** running towards the left. The origin of this statue is not certain, it has been thought to be an acroterion from the Doric treasury in the sanctuary of Athena Pronaia (no. 6), but it may also belong to a sculptural group carved in the round.

Hymn in honour of Apollo (no. 1).

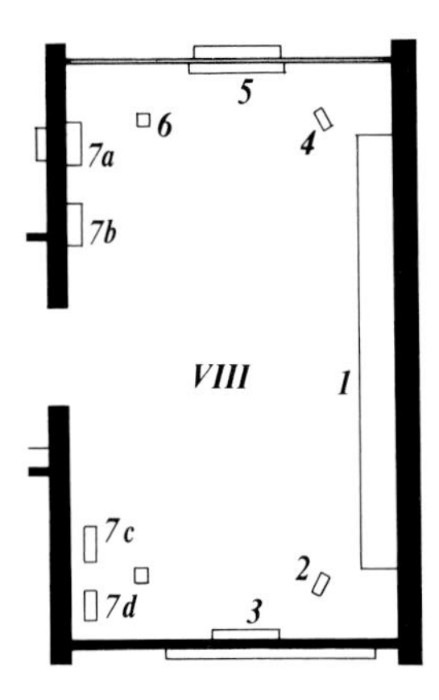

ROOM VIII: 'Temple of Apollo Room'

The main exhibit in this room is the **east pediment of the 'temple of the Alcmaeonidae' (1)**, which can be seen on the wall just opposite the entrance of room VIII (coming from room VII). As mentioned above, this pediment was made of Parian marble. The pedimental sculpture is fragmentary, but preserves traces of colour. It represents the arrival of Apollo at Delphi. The god in a chariot must have been at the centre and was probably accompanied by his mother Leto and his sister Artemis. The composition was flanked by scenes of animal fights at the corners.

On the right, as we face the pediment, is a **winged figure (2)** wearing a chiton and himation. This is a Nike who might have been the central acroterion of the temple. Next to the Nike is **part of the sima (3)** from the 'temple of the Alcmaeonidae' decorated with a lion head at the edge.

Female statue from the east pediment of the 'temple of the Alcmaeonidae' (no. 1).

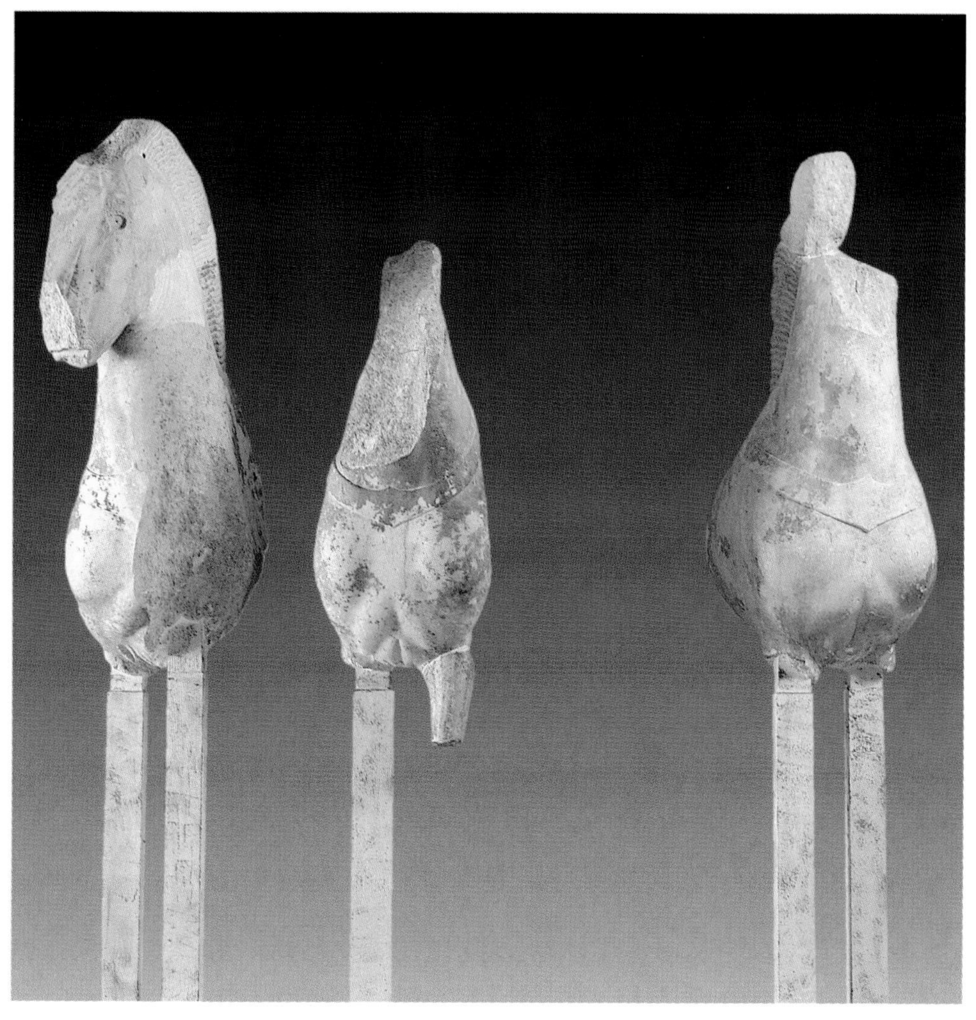

Fragments of the horses from the chariot of Apollo on the east pediment of the 'temple of the Alcmaeonidae' (no. 1).

At the left of the pedimental sculpture is a **statue of Dionysus (4)**. The god is presented with a beard, wearing a short girt chiton. The square hole close to his left arm was probably for supporting an additional object, such as a lyre. Thus, this statue of Dionysus was probably made according to the sculptural type of Apollo. This figure of Dionysus has been associated with the west pediment of the temple of Apollo which is dated to the 4th century BC (340-330 BC), because Pausanias (X,19,4-5) describes Dionysus among the women of his thiasos, the Thyades, on this pediment. Next to the statue is **part of the sima (5)** from the same temple.

On the left, as we face the exit of room VIII towards room VII, there is a **statue of a seated figure (6)**. It is dressed in a chiton and has a himation folded on the knees. The rear surface is unfinished which suggests that it was not visible. This may be the statue of Apollo which stood at the centre of the east pediment of the 4th century temple, and possibly depicted the god holding a kithara. However, the original position of the

Statue of Nike, possible an acroterion from the 'temple of the Alcmaeonidae' (no. 2).

Statue of Dionysus, 340-330 BC (no. 4).

Statue of a seated figure, (Apollo?), 4th century BC (no. 6).

statue is not certain and it has also been suggested that it may have stood in one of the niches in the pronaos of Apollo's temple.

Marble inscribed stelai (7 a-d) are exhibited on both sides of the exit. The inscriptions refer to financial matters relating to the oracle, such as the expenses for restoring the temple of Apollo in the spring of 361 BC, in 358-342 BC and 341-310 BC. Finally, on the stele to the left of the exit (7 c) is inscribed the fine imposed on the Phocians at the end of the Third Sacred War, in 346 BC.

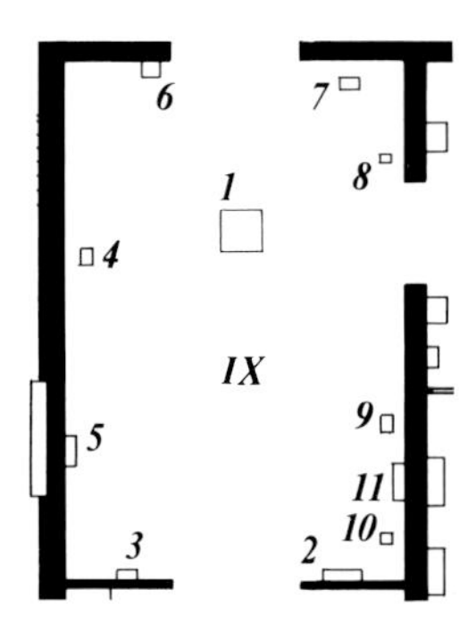

ROOM IX:
'Funerary Stele Room'

The entrance to room IX is from room VII. At the centre of this room is a **circular altar (1)** made of pentelic marble which was found in the sanctuary of Athena Pronaia. The altar stood on a rectangular pedestal which has also been preserved. The altar is dated in the 2nd century BC and is decorated with twelve female figures arranged in couples, who are shown attaching ribbons to the floral band carved along its upper surface.

On either side of the entrance and the altar are three grave stelai. The oldest **(no. 2)** was probably produced in the islands and is dated around the second quarter of the 5th century BC; the stele is broken, and on the preserved fragment a man is depicted wrapped in a long himation, turning to the right and resting on a stick. The second **stele (3)** is probably dated in the middle of the

Detail from the decoration of the marble altar from the sanctuary of Athena Pronaia (no. 1).

5th century BC and represents a young woman holding a mirror. The last **stele (4)** is decorated with two frontal figures, a youth (ephebe) accompanied by his young assistant. The latter was holding a vessel in his left hand, of which only the handle has been preserved. The former possibly had his arms positioned according to the sculptural type of the Apoxyomenos: with a strigil in one hand he was scraping the oil from his body. If this reconstruction is correct, then the vessel held by the young escort was probably an aryballos, the oil container used by athletes to anoint their body for the athletic contests which took place at the palaestra. A notable detail is the head of a dog between the two figures. This stele was made either in the islands or in Ionia and is dated around the middle of the 5th century BC.

To the left of the grave stele is a **showcase (5)** holding Attic clay vases (e.g. lekythoi), glass vessels (e.g. alabastra and amphoriskoi), as well as a miniature pyxis made of ivory. Most of these vases are dated to the 5th century BC

Marble altar from the sanctuary of Athena Pronaia, 2nd century BC (no. 1).

and were found in graves, which confirms that objects of everyday use were also placed in graves as offerings.
On the left side of the exit leading to room XI is a **relief (6)** dated in the late 5th century BC with a representation of a horse from a four-horsed chariot. On the right-hand side of this exit is a **marble statue (7)** of the god Apollo in the type of the kitharodos; it is 93 cm high and is dated to the 3rd century BC.
As we continue walking to the right we encounter a **statue (8) dated to the 4th century BC**. It represents a woman running; her vigorous movement is reflected in her dress which clings to her body and reveals its outline as if she was naked. It has been suggested that this figure was one of the acroteria of the tholos in the sanctuary of Athena Pronaia (no. 9), but there is insufficient evidence to confirm this theory.
The following exhibits are **two bronze hydrias (9, 10)** and between them **clay female busts (11)**. The hydrias are dated to the middle of the 5th century BC and were used as funerary urns for carrying the ashes of the deceased after the cremation. The female busts may represent the goddess Demeter and her daughter, Persephone.

Funerary stele, c. 450 BC (no. 4).

Right: Statue of Apollo in the type of kitharodos, c. 3rd century BC (no. 7).

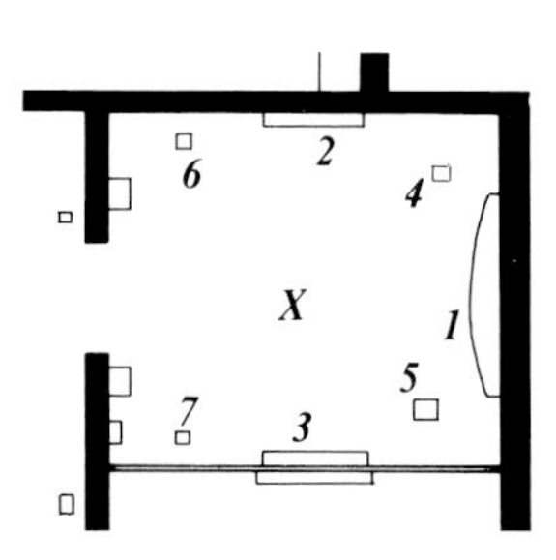

ROOM X:
'Tholos Room'

The right exit from room IX leads us to the next room, where the sculpture from the tholos (no. 9 in the sanctuary of Athena Pronaia) is exhibited. As mentioned above, the tholos had an exterior peristyle with twenty columns and an interior colonnade with ten columns. These circular colonnades carried a Doric frieze, with triglyphs and metopes carved in high relief.

On the wall **(1)** opposite the entrance to this room, as well as in the central **show-cases (2, 3)** attached to the wall on either side of the entrance, are exhibited the fragments from the metopes of the tholos. The large metopes supported by the exterior colonnade depicted an Amazonomachy and a Centauromachy. The Amazons and the Centaurs were mythological creatures, who were differentiated from human beings by their life style and their appearance (for the Amazons

Female statue, possibly acroterion of the tholos.

Amazons from the metopes on the exterior peristyle of the tholos (show-cases nos. 1-3).

see p. 106-109). The Centaurs were wild beasts with a human torso attached to the body of a horse. They acted instinctively and neglected any kind of human laws. The most famous Centauromachy in Greek art was the one that was supposed to have taken place at the wedding of Peirithous; the Centaurs intruded upon the wedding feast and abducted the wives of the guests. Theseus is one of the main protagonists in this story because he was the dearest friend of the groom; together with Peirithous he defended the safety of the bride. The victory of humans against the Centaurs signifies the superiority of civilised human forces over the lawless and barbarian elements in nature and society. The metopes above the interior colonnade were smaller and are preserved in fragments; they were most probably decorated with episodes from the labours of Heracles and Theseus.

The **female statues (4, 5, 6, 7)**, standing on either side of the show-cases (nos 2 and 3), were probably the acroteria of the tholos. They are dressed in garments with rich folds, which cling to the body and reveal its naked forms underneath. These statues are characteristic examples of the so-called 'Rich or Ornate Style' which flourished at the end of the 5th and the beginning of the 4th century BC.

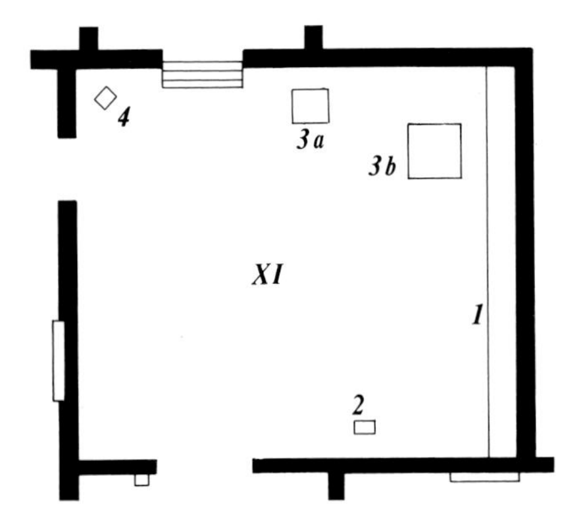

ROOM XI:
'Monument of Daochus Room'
(see p. 55-56, no. 66)

To the right of the entrance we see the **monument of Daochus (1)** and **one of its statues (2)**, which stands separately on the right. According to the votive inscription preserved on the pedestal, the monument was dedicated by Daochus II, the Thessalian tetrarch who served as hieromnenon at the Delphic Amphictyony between 339-334 BC, when he must have made this dedication. It is a monumental offering of particular interest and significance, because it was dedicated by an individual and not by a city like most of the other offerings. The intention of Daochus II must have been to honour his family and his country as well as himself.

The archaeological evidence suggests that this monument was placed in a rectangular exedra and stood on a pedestal holding nine statues made of Parian marble. The name of each figure and praise of his virtues were inscribed on the pedestal below each statue. Not all the statues are preserved intact. They have been attributed to the monument according to the following factors: 1) their find place, 2) on the site similarities in the quality of the marble, 3) their size and style, and 4) the correlation between the plinths they are standing on and the holes on the pedestal.

The name of the first figure, as we face the pedestal on the right, is not preserved. Some scholars believe that here was a seated statue of Apollo holding the kithara (in the type of the kitharodos), because he was the god honoured in the sanctuary. Alternatively, a statue of Athena has also been suggested, because she was supposed to be the patron-goddess of Thessaly, the city of Daochus II. The remaining statues represented the predecessors and descendants of Daochus II according to age sequence: Acnonius, Agias, Telemachus, Agelaus, Daochus I, Sisiphus I, Daochus II, and finally Sisyphus II.

One should note the variety of postures as well as the differentiation in the rendering of movements and garments, according to the age of each figure. Acnonius is wearing a short chiton and himation. Daochus I is dressed in the heavy Thessalian chlamys, which is long enough to reach the knee level and gives him the image of a noble landowner. Sisyphus I is also fully dressed with a girt chiton and a himation falling over his arm. The strap of his scabbard is shown on his chest; this detail alludes to his military activities which are also praised in the epigram on the pedestal. Finally, the sandals preserved from the statue of Daochus II suggest that this figure was also dressed. Telemachus (standing to the right of the pedestal, no. 2), Agelaus and Sisyphus II are depicted naked,

Statue of Acnonius from the monument of Daochus (no. 1).

Statue of Daochus I from the monument of Daochus (no. 1).

but their bodies are not as strongly built as the body of Agias, the best preserved statue of the monument. Agias is presented as a naked youth resting on his right leg. Although the statue of Agias is not a portrait but an idealised picture of an athlete, it possesses some degree of individuality suggested by his lively posture, the expression of passion on his face and the upright position of his head.

To the left of this pedestal is the so-called **column of the dancing girls (3a-b)**, which stood in the area to the north-east of the temple of Apollo (see p. 56-57, no. 68). We see here part of the column (3a) crowned by a capital with acanthus leaves. A group of three women, each one with her right arm raised, was supported by the column capital. The female figures were probably dancers holding a tripod with a cauldron on their heads. The bottom drum of the column (3b) is placed next to 3a and is also decorated with leaves of acanthus. This monument was made of pentelic marble and was probably the work of an Ionian artist of the 4th century BC.

At the opposite corner is the **statue of an elderly man (4)** with a himation leaving his breast exposed. It is an original marble statue dated around 280-270 BC. His garment and posture suggest he is either a philosopher or a priest of Apollo.

Statue of Sisiphus I from the monument of Daochus (no.1).

Statue of the runner Agelaus from the monument of Daochus (no. 1).

Statue of Sisiphos II from the monument of Daochus (no. 1).

Statue of the athlete Agias from the monument of Daochus (no. 1).

Right: The 'column of the dancing girls', 4th century BC (no. 3a).

Statue of an elderly man wearing a himation, 280-270 BC (no. 4).

Torso of the statue of Telemachus from the monument of Daochus (no. 2).

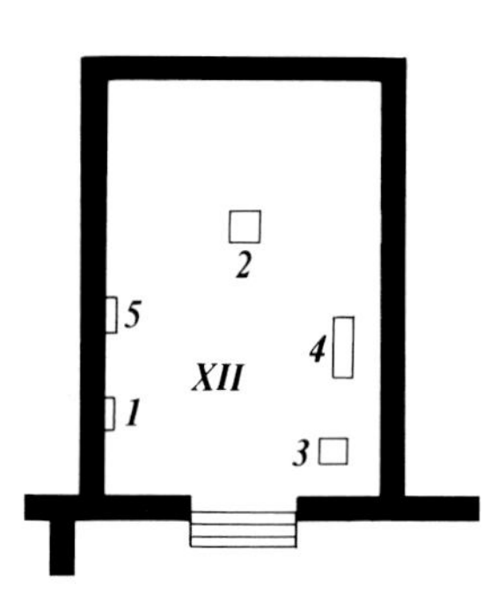

ROOM XII:
'Charioteer Room'

As we enter the room we first see on the left an **attic cup (kylix) (1)**, a drinking vessel found in a grave. It is dated to c. 480 BC and has been attributed to the Berlin Painter. It is decorated in a distinctive manner: the figure of Apollo is drawn against a white background. The god is identified by the lyre in his left hand; he is seated on a stool with crossed legs, and pours a libation from a bowl in his right hand. The scene takes place in the presence of a bird, identified by some scholars as the crow that announced to Apollo the wedding of his beloved Coronis. According to the myth, the bad news made Apollo very angry and as a result he cursed the crow to become as black as was the colour of his heart. However, H. Metzger believes that this scene does not allude to any particular myth, but simply shows Apollo accompanied by a bird of prediction.

The remaining exhibits in this room are contemporary with the cup and belong to the votive offering of Gelon or Polyzalus (see p. 60, no. 71). The centre of the room is dominated by the **bronze charioteer (2)**. The young charioteer holds the reins in his right hand and wears a long chiton, fastened so that it would be restrained at high speeds,

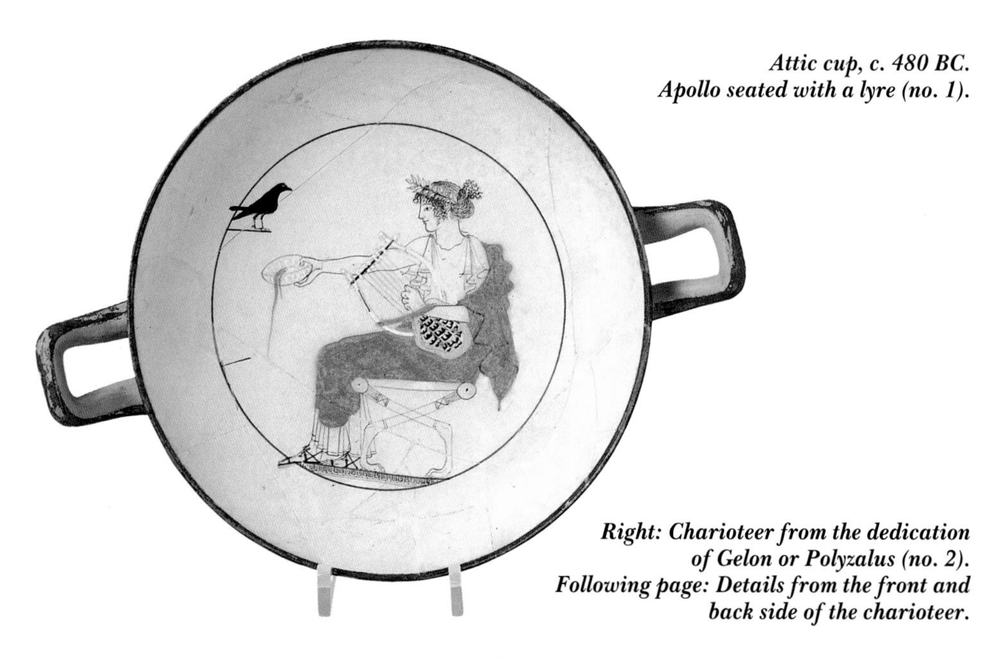

Attic cup, c. 480 BC. Apollo seated with a lyre (no. 1).

Right: Charioteer from the dedication of Gelon or Polyzalus (no. 2). Following page: Details from the front and back side of the charioteer.

with a girdle below his chest which forms two diagonal stripes at the back. His head is turned slightly to the left and its features are rendered in great detail: his eyes are inlaid pieces made of glass and stone, his hairband is silver plated and finally his lips were accentuated by red-coloured copper. It is a typical work of the so-called Severe Style, which flourished in the early Classical period (475-450 BC).

The other fragments attributed to this monument are exhibited around the charioteer: **part of the base (3)**, on which traces of the votive inscription are preserved; **parts of the chariot, the reins, and the horse's legs (4)**, and the **left forearm of a young child (5)**. These finds suggest that the charioteer should probably be pictured standing in a four-horsed chariot following a horse accompanied by a young boy.

Detail from the bronze statue of the charioteer. The hand holding the reins (no. 2).

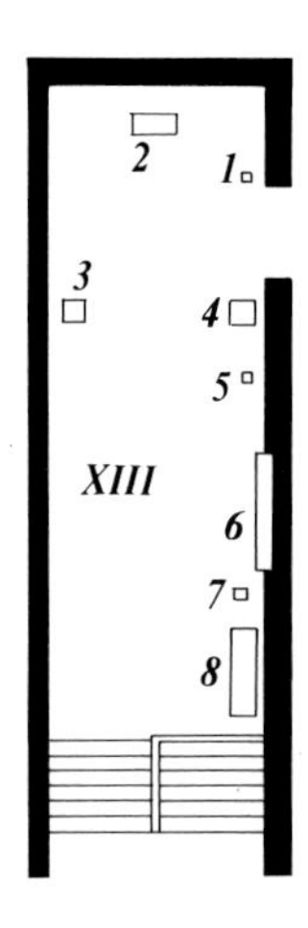

ROOM XIII:
'Antinous Room'

We return to room XI in order to visit the last room of the museum. As we enter room XIII, on the right, we encounter the **marble statue of a young boy with a goose (1)**. The statue may have been either an individual dedication or part of a larger sculptural group. The iconographic scheme of a child with a bird became very popular in the 3rd century BC.

The famous **statue of Antinous (2)**, on the left, is made of Parian marble and is dated to c. 130-138 AD. It is a remarkable portrait that demonstrates the development of portraiture since the Hellenistic period. Antinous was a beloved friend of the emperor Hadrian, who honoured him after his death by introducing his cult at Delphi and erecting his statue in several sanctuaries. The statue in the museum of Delphi represents Antinous as a handsome naked young man with long hair decorated with a wreath. His head is slightly bent downwards and to the right, a movement reflecting his sobriety, while his look is absorbed as he gazes into infinity.

We walk towards the left. First, we see a **marble bust of a bearded man (3)**, which probably originally stood on a Hermaic stele. Its facial characteristics may be attributed to the portrait of a philosopher dated to the 3rd century BC.

Marble bust of a bearded man, 3rd century BC (no. 3).

Opposite is the **statue of a young woman (4)** wearing a girt chiton and himation. The figure rests on her left leg, while the slight bend of her right leg is reflected in the rest of her body. Stylistically the statue is dated to the 3rd century BC; it and the statue of a young boy (1), which we saw at the entrance to this room, are representative examples

Marble head of a man, possible the Roman Titus Flamininus (no. 7).

Statue of a young woman, 3rd century BC (no. 4).

of the popularity of child iconography in the Hellenistic period.

Next to no. 4 is a **Hermaic stele (5)** holding a marble bust of Plutarch (46-126 AD), the historian who served a double priesthood at Delphi.

On the right-hand side is a **show-case (6) with objects from Cirrha**, close to modern Itea, which was the ancient port of Crisa. Excavations in the area have discovered a sanctuary, most probably dedicated to the Delian Triad - Apollo, Artemis and Leto- which must have been in use from the 6th to the 4th century BC. The objects in this showcase were most probably votive offerings to this sanctuary and are mainly small vases such as cups, skyphoi, hydrias, kraters, as well as clay female busts.

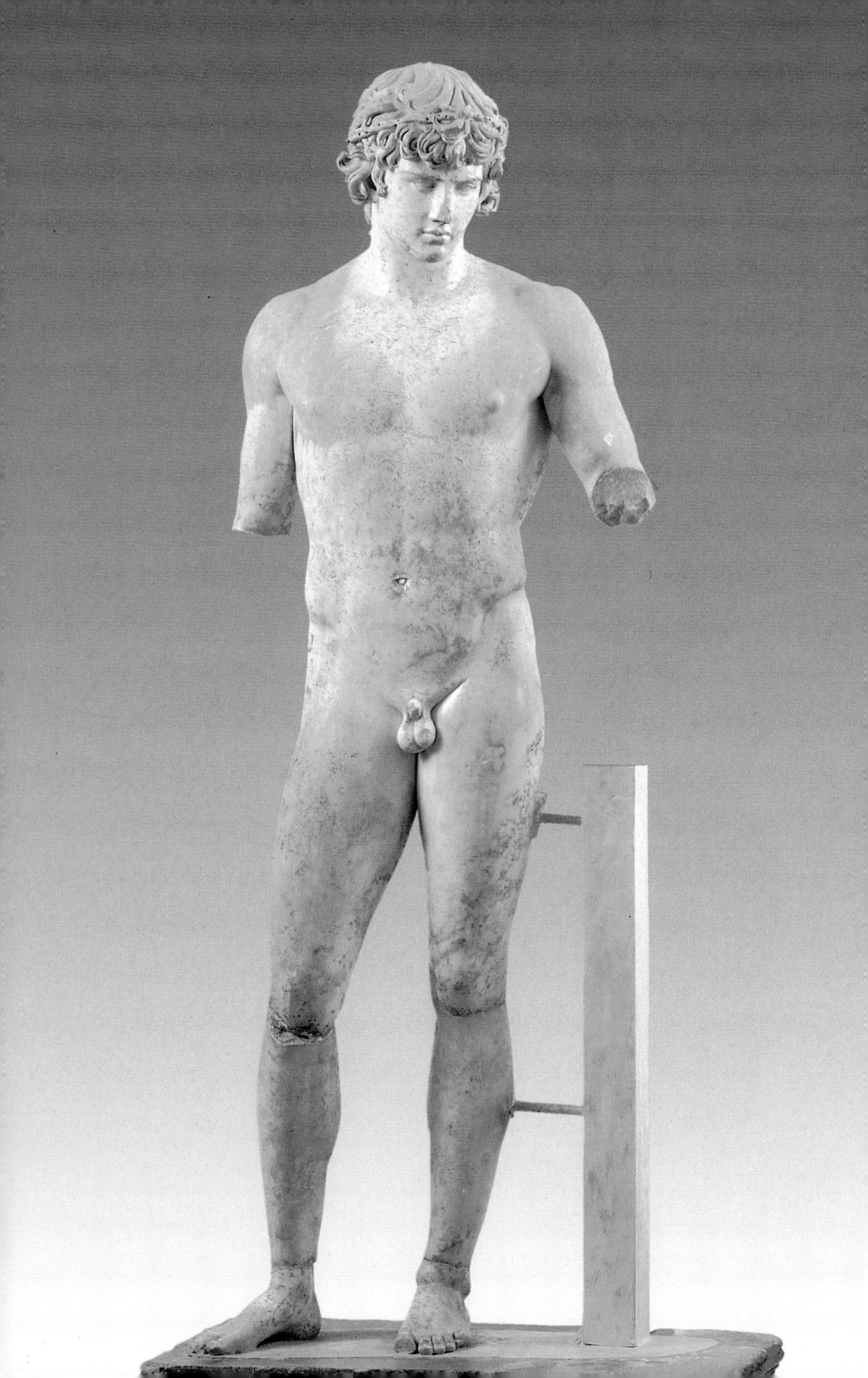

Statue of Antinous, AD 130-138 (no. 2).

Attic clay plaque with a Dionysiac scene and votive inscription, 525-500 BC (show-case 8).

Next to the show-case **is a male head (7)** made of Parian marble. Its features suggest that it was a portrait, which, according to some scholars, is identified with the Roman Titus Flamininus, who defeated the king of Macedon, Philip V, at Cynoscephalae in 197 BC.

Finally, in the last show-case **(8) are exhibited the finds from the Corycian Cave**. The testimonies of Pausanias and the geographer Strabo as well as inscriptions carved on stones and vessels found in the area, identify the Corycian Cave as a sacred cave in the foothills of Parnassus dedicated to the god Pan and the Nymphs. Small finds confirm the use of the cave for cult practices from the 8th century BC until the 2nd century AD, while the sanctuary flourished between the 6th and the 2nd century BC. Various objects have been discovered in the cave, such as a large number of clay vases and figurines, offerings made of bronze, iron and glass, as well as fragments of bases from marble statues. Most interesting is an Attic clay plaque which is dated in the last quarter of the 6th century BC and is decorated with satyrs and maenads dancing. The letters (...ΦΑΙΣ) of the votive inscription, still visible on the left part of the plaque, confirm that the object was dedicated to the Nymphs. Another important find is also made of clay and presents twelve Nymphs in a circle around Pan, who plays the double-

Clay wheel holding twelve Nymphs around Pan, circa 450 BC (show-case 8).

flute. The figures are standing on a base in the shape of a wheel and the women are placed symmetrically, three on each quadrant. This was most probably made by a Boeotian workshop around the middle of the 5th century BC. The association of Pan and the Nymphs with music is attested by both this monument and the ivory flute, also found in this cave and exhibited here.

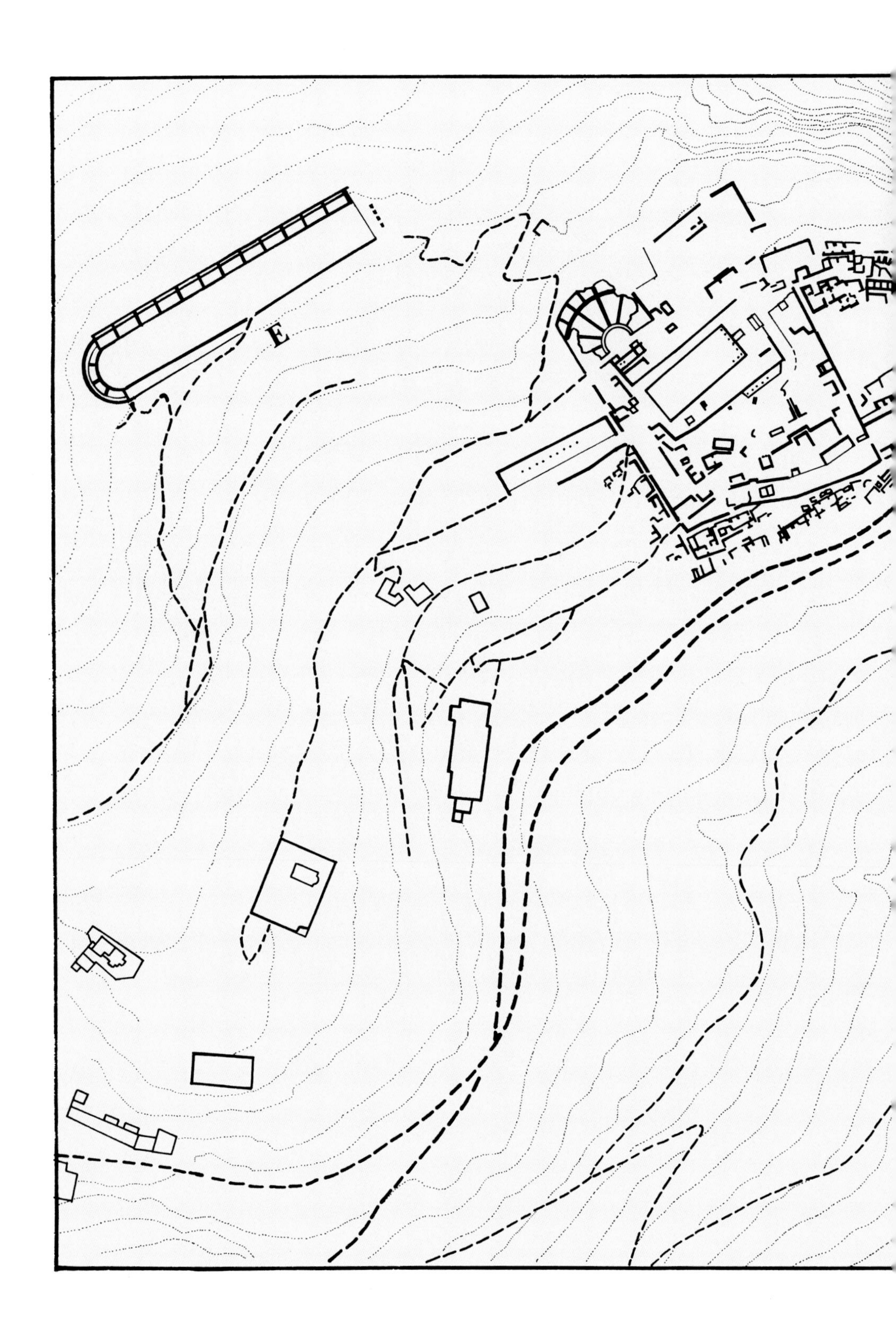
E

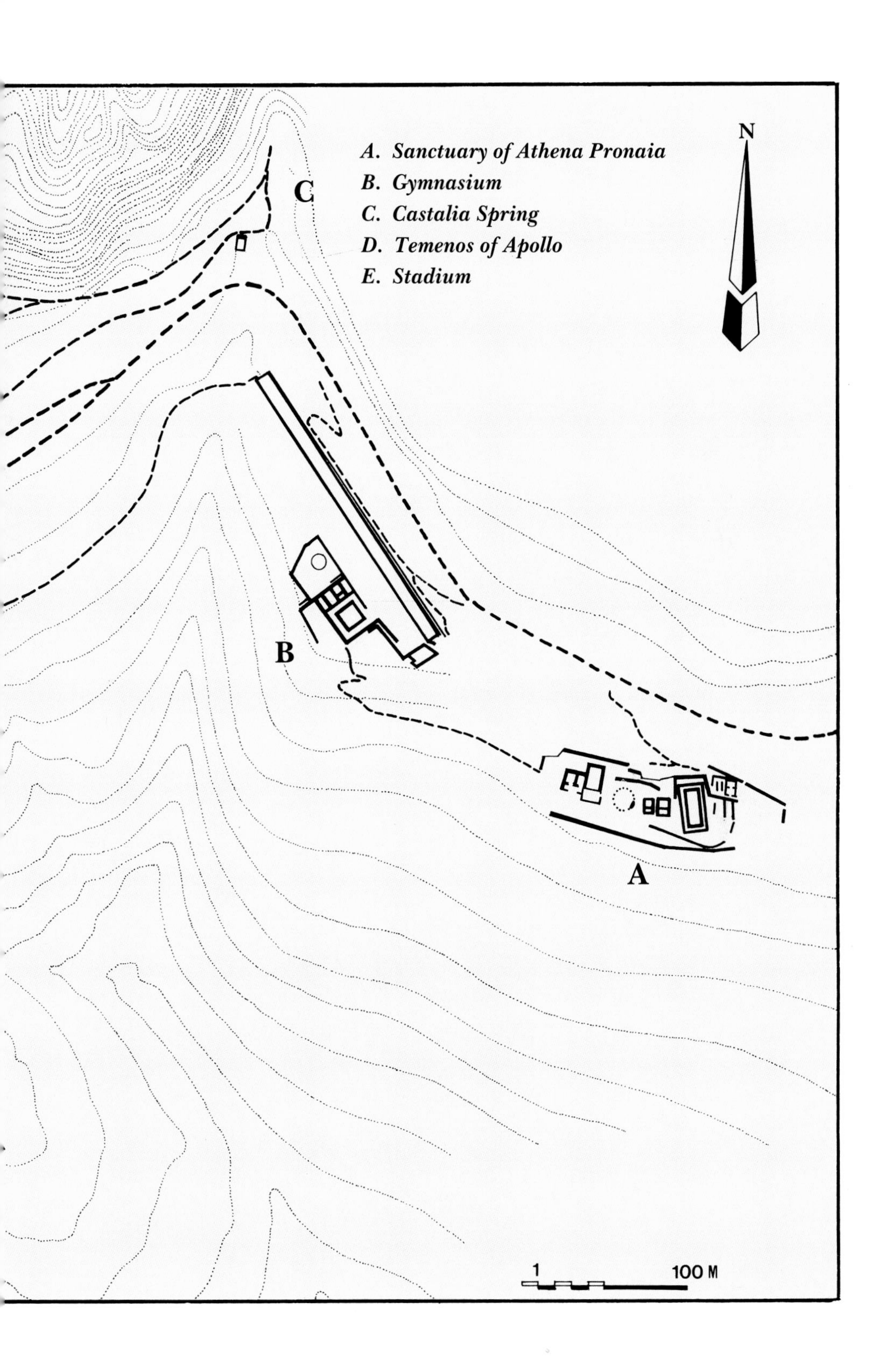
A. Sanctuary of Athena Pronaia
B. Gymnasium
C. Castalia Spring
D. Temenos of Apollo
E. Stadium
N
C
B
A
1
100 M

14th-11th cent. BC	11th-9th cent. BC	7th cent. BC	Middle of 7th cent BC	650-630 BC
Mycenaean settlement.	Introduction of the cult of Apollo at Delphi.	Foundation of the Delphic Amphictyony.	Building of the first temple of Apollo, which was made of limestone. Pausanias (X,5,13) mentions Trophonius and Agemedes as the architects.	The first temple of Athena Pronaia is built.

600-590 BC	586 BC	582 BC	548-7 BC	514-505 BC	500-479 BC

586 BC: The Amphictyony decides to include competitions of flute-playing and singing to the accompaniment of a flute-player in the Pythian Games.

582 BC:

Athletic contests are added to the Pythian Games. The contests are similar to those held in the Olympic Games except for the omission of the four-horse chariot race and the boy's dolichos (α long-distance foot-race). The singing to the accompaniment of flute-playing is abolished, while the chariot race is introduced.

548-7 BC: The temple of Apollo is destroyed by a fire.

600-590 BC: First Sacred War. The Amphictyony declares war against the city of Crisa. The reason was the attempt of Crisa to exact a kind of tribute from the pilgrims who disembarked at its port, Cirrha. The war resulted in the victory of Delphi and the destruction of both Crisa and Cirrha. The city of Delphi is declared to be independent in the Amphictyony and maintains its rights to have full control of the oracle and to choose the priests of Apollo only from its inhabitants.
Organisation of the Pythian Games; they were celebrated every four years and a laurel wreath was the prize for the victors. At the beginning they involved only musical competitions in the performance of the kithara.
Second temple of Athena Pronaia.

514-505 BC: The next temple of Apollo is constructed. The building is financed by the Alcmaeonidae and the east façade is made of marble.

500-479 BC: Persian Wars

The Persians fail to invade and plunder the oracle. To commemorate the event the city of Delphi erects a trophy in the sanctuary of Athena Pronaia. The earlier level of the altar of Apollo is also dated to the first half of the 5th century BC.

The Tholos in the sanctuary of Athena Pronaia is built.

Third temple of Athena Pronaia.

480 BC	448 π.Χ.	421 BC	Beginning of 4th cent. BC	373-2 BC	Around 350 BC

The Delphic oracle regains its independence and is freed from its commitment to the city of Phocis.

The temple of Apollo (the so-called temple of the Alcmaeonidae) is destroyed by an earthquake. Soon afterwards the architect Spintharus is assigned to rebuilt it.

Second Sacred War. The city of Delphi is involved in a defensive war against the Phocians who had occupied territories in the possession of the Delphic oracle. First, the Phocians were expelled by the Lacedaemonians, but later they managed to return with the assistance of the Athenians and undertake the responsibilty for the organisation of the Pythian Games.

Third Sacred War. Delphi is again involved in a defensive war against the Phocians who had attempted once again to violate and cultivate territories in the possession of the oracle. The Phocians occupy the sanctuary until 346 BC and take many of the votive offerings, such as the gold tripod dedicated for the victory at the battle of Plataea (see p. 50, no. 41). The restoration of Apollo's temple is interrupted.

Philip II, the king of Macedon, interferes and puts an end to the Third Sacred War. The Phocians are penalised with a fine and the loss of their voting rights at the meetings of the Amphictyony.

The Gauls invade Delphi. Their advance is held with the assistance of the Aetolians. The 'Soteria' is inaugurated; it is an annual festival celebrated in the autumn, during which musical, lyrical and drama contests take place.

356-346 BC	346 BC	339-338 BC	330-29 BC	279 BC	246 BC

Fourth Sacred War. The city of Delphi fights the Locrians who invaded the plain of Crisa. Philip II destroys the city of the Locrians and defeats the Athenians and the Thebans at the battle of Chaironeia.

The restoration of the temple of Apollo is completed.

It is decided that the festival of the 'Soteria' will be celebrated every five years in the honour of Zeus Soter (the Saviour) and Apollo and that it will be as prestigious as the Pythian Games.

191-168 BC	159 BC	86 BC	83 BC	AD 67	AD 84

191-168 BC: The sanctuary is occupied by the Romans after the victory of Aemilius Paulus against Perseus, the king of Macedon, at Pydna in 168 BC.

159 BC: Eumenes II, king of Pergamon, finances the building of a monumental structure at the theatre.

86 BC: The sanctuary is invaded and plundered by Sulla, who takes many of the gold and silver offerings.

83 BC: Invasion of barbarians from Thrace at Delphi. The flame that had burnt for centuries in the hearth of the temple is extinguished and the building is badly damaged.

AD 67: The Roman emperor Nero, takes part in the Pythian Games and loots 500 statues from the sanctuary. The plain of Crisa falls into the hands of his veterans.

AD 84: Domitian orders the restoration of some parts of Apollo's temple.

The fame of the oracle is temporarily revived by the emperor Hadrian who introduces the cult of his friend Antinous. In addition, Hadrian gives several orders for repairs in the sanctuary and attempts to re-establish the Amphictyony.

Herodes Atticus finances the construction of stone seats at the stadium of Delphi.

Theodosius the Great issues a decree forbidding all pagan cults. As a result the oracle of Apollo is sealed for ever and the Pythian Games are suspended.

AD 120	AD 125-130	AD 394	End of 6th - beginning of 7th cent. AD

Invasion of the Slavs.

The hot baths are built at the Gymnasium.

TARAS
CORCYRA
SICILY
SYRACUSE
M E D I T E R R A N E

MACEDONIA
ACANTHUS
PERCAMON
AITOLIA
DELPHI
THEBES
CHIOS
ACHAIA
SICYON
CORINTH
ATHENS
ARGOS
ARCADIA
SPARTA
SIPHNOS
NAXOS
CNIDUS
RHODES
A
CYRENE

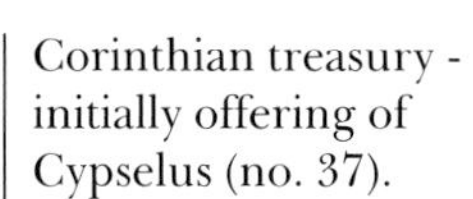

Corinthian treasury - initially offering of Cypselus (no. 37).

Treasury of Cnidus (no. 24).

Siphnian treasury (no. 14).

657-628 BC	570-560 BC	550-544 BC	530-525 BC	Around 500 BC

Naxian sphinx (no. 33).

Athenian treasury (no. 21).

Treasury of Sicyon (no. 13).

Votive offering of the Athenians for the victory at the battle of Marathon (no. 22).

Athenian stoa (no. 34).

Bronze bull - dedication of the people of Corcyra (no. 1).

Dedication of the city of Delphi in the sanctuary of Athena Pronaia (no. 8) in the memory of the repelling of the Persian army.

Bronze statues of women on horses - offering of Taras (no. 12).

500-475 BC	500-450 BC	After 490 BC	Around 490-465 BC	After 480 BC

Altar of Apollo - offering of the Chians (no. 44).

Bronze statues - Athenian offering (no. 6).

Gold tripods - offering of the Deinomenids (no. 58)

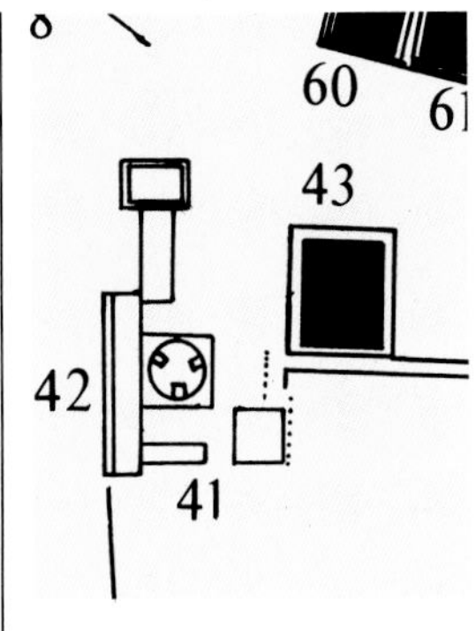

Gold tripod dedicated from the spoils of the battle of Plataea (no. 41).

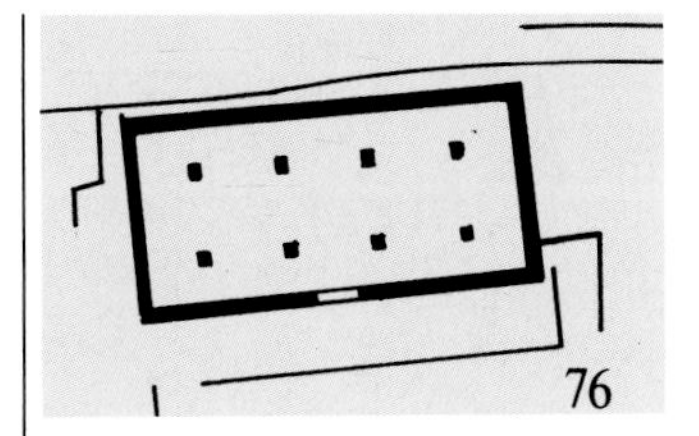

Lesche of the Cnidians (no. 76).

After 479 BC	Around 478-470 BC	Around 475-460 BC	After 465 BC

Bronze palm-tree and gilt image of Athena - Athenian offering (no. 55).

Group with the bronze charioteer - offered by a tyrant of Gela in Sicily (no. 71).

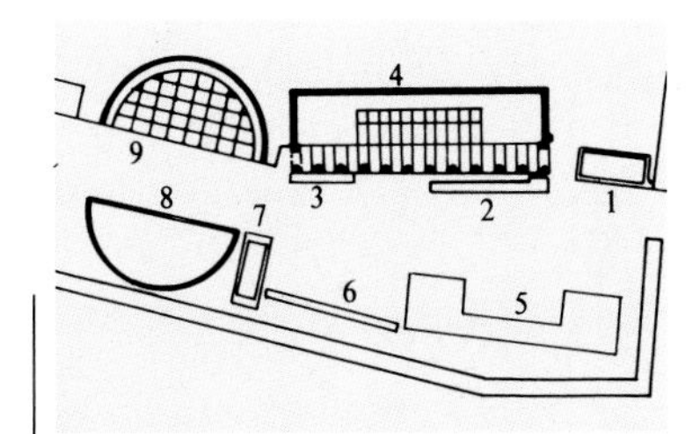

Bronze statues of the Seven against Thebes and the Epigonoi - Argive offering (no. 8).

Bronze statue of the Trojan Horse - offering of Argos (no. 7).

After 456 BC	After 423 BC	After 414 BC	After 413 BC	After 404 BC

Treasury of the city of Acanthus and Brasidas (no. 40).

Bronze statues of gods and heroes - Spartan offering (no. 5).

Treasury of Syracuse (no. 26).

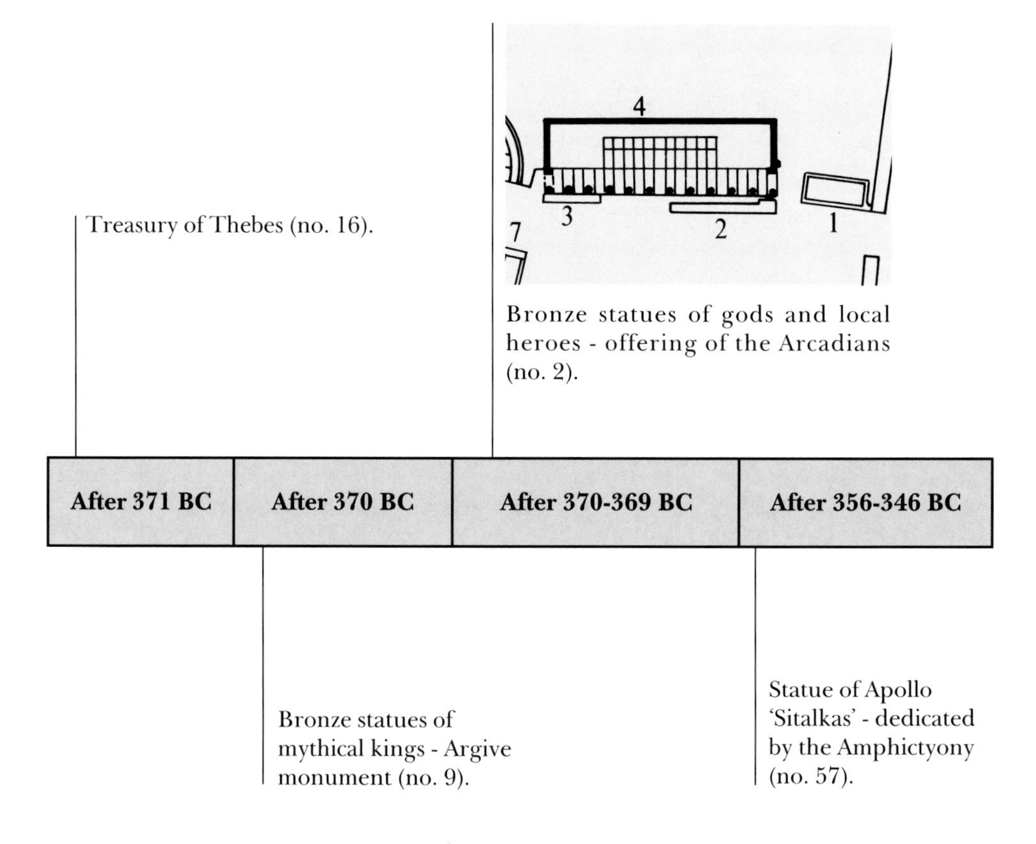
Treasury of Thebes (no. 16).
4
3
2
1
7
Bronze statues of gods and local heroes - offering of the Arcadians (no. 2).
After 371 BC
After 370 BC
After 370-369 BC
After 356-346 BC
Bronze statues of mythical kings - Argive monument (no. 9).
Statue of Apollo 'Sitalkas' - dedicated by the Amphictyony (no. 57).

334-322-1 BC	330 BC.	320-300 BC	Around 304 BC	After 279 BC

'column of the dancing girls' - offering of the Athenians (no. 68).

Gilded chariot of the god Helios (Sun) - monument of the Rhodians (no. 43).

Treasury of Cyrene (no. 38a).

Dedication of Craterus (no. 78).

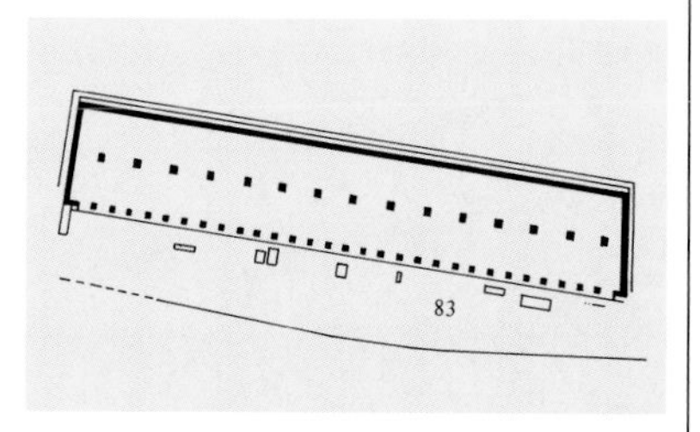

Stoa of the Aetolians (no. 82).

Statue of Prusias II - offering of the Aetolian League (no. 56).

Statue of Eunenes II - dedication of the Aetolian League (no. 45).

Statues of Attalus I and Eumenes II - offerings of the Amphictyony (nos 60, 61).

Statue of Aemilius Paulus (no. 47).

Around 220 BC	197-182 BC	182 BC	After 183 BC	After 168 BC	159-138 BC

Bronze statue of Philopoemen - dedication of the Achaean League (no. 3).

Statue of Attalus II - dedication of the city of Delphi (in front of no. 34).

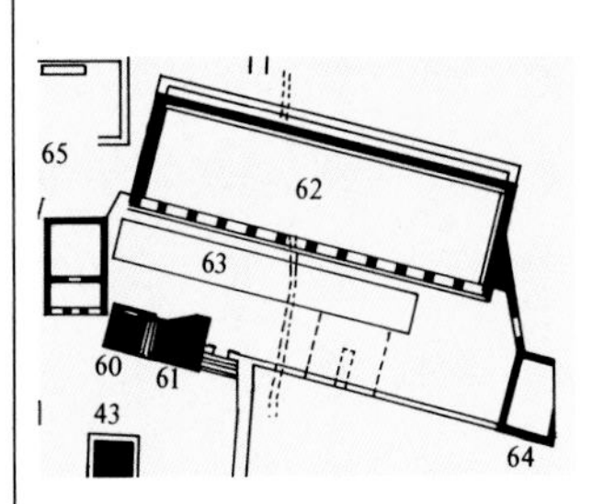

Stoa of Attalus I (no. 62).

14th - 11th cent. BC	Mycenaean period
11th - 9th cent. BC	'Dark Ages'
9th - 7th cent. BC	Geometric period Early: 900 - 850 BC Middle: 850 - 770 BC Late: 770 - 700 BC
7th - 6th cent. BC	Archaic period Early: 700 - 600 BC Middle: 600 - 530 BC Late: 530 - 480 BC
5th - mid 4th cent. BC	Classical period Early: 480 - 450 BC Middle: 450 - 400 BC Late: 400 - 330 BC
336 - 168 BC	Hellenistic period
168 BC - 300 AD	Roman period
300 AD - 1453 AD	Byzantine period

Acroterion
Statue standing on the corner of the pediment.

Adyton
An enclosed area inside the cella of a temple. It was a sacred room, which was occasionally used as a treasury.

Acrothinion
First-fruits of the field, booty etc., offered to the gods.

Aeolic capital
An early type of column capital shaped like a palm-tree. It was introduced from north-western Asia Minor.

Altar
A sacred area or structure, usually in front of the eastern entrance of a temple, where sacrificial rituals in honour of the god were performed.

Amazons
Mythical female warriors from Asia Minor, said to have fought against Heracles and Theseus.

Amphictyony
A committee formed by cities joined together in a kind of religious union for supporting their rights. In antiquity the Delphic Amphictyony was the most important. Its meetings were held in the autumn at Anthele, a city close to Thermopylae, and in the spring at Delphi.

Anta
The protruding part at the end of a wall.

Architrave
The architectural member carried by two capitals; it is placed so that its edges were aligned with the centre of each capital.

Aryballos
Vase of spherical shape. It was usually small and contained olive oil or perfumed oil which was used mainly by athletes at the Gymnasium.

Caryatid
Statue of a standing female figure in frontal position, which could be used as an architectural member instead of a column.

Cauldron
Open vessel of spherical shape, wich was often carried on a tripod. It was used for serving wine, although metal cauldrons were usually presented as offerings to sanctuaries.

Cella
The central part of a temple, between the pronaos and the opisthodomos, where the cult statue was placed.

Column
Fluted shaft. There are two types of columns: the Doric, which does not have a base and is characterised by its heavy and bulky proportions and the Ionic, which has an elaborately decorated base and is slender and finer.

Column capital
The part crowning a column. The most common types of capitals are: the Doric, the Ionic and the Corinthian.

Cornice
The lower part of the roof of a temple, above the entablature; it is projecting and holds the antefixes from which flows the rainwater.

Cyma
A decorative moulding, which is alternatively convex and concave.

Diaulos
A double-length of the stadium foot-race; the finishing point was the same as the starting point.

Doric frieze
A decorative band with triglyphs and metopes, which was carried by the architrave.

Doric order
An architectural order which seems to be particularly popular in Mainland Greece and the Doric colonies. Its main characteristics are its heavy and bulky proportions.

Drum
One of the cylindrical parts of a column shaft.

Echinos
The convex part of a Doric column capital.

Entablature
The architectural parts of a temple carried by the columns; it consists of the architrave, the frieze and the cornice.

Figurine
A statue of small size (statuette) presenting a human or an animal figure. It can be made of clay, bronze or marble.

Hermaic stele (pl. stelai)
A stele in the shape of a rectangular pillar crowned by the protome (bust) of a bearded Hermes. Such monuments were used as sign posts in antiquity, marking street directions. In late antiquity Hermaic stelai could be used as support pillars for the busts of famous men.

Hieromnemon
The representative of each city-member of the Delphic Amphictyony.

Ionic frieze
A continuous decorative band with representations in relief.

Ionic order
An architectural order developed mainly in the islands and Asia Minor. Its main characteristics are its slender and tall proportions.

Kithara
Stringed musical instrument, similar to the lyre. It was used mainly by highly experienced musicians, such as the god of music, Apollo himself. It was also played by music teachers and its performance formed part of musical contests.

Kouros
Marble statue of a male figure in frontal position. It has one leg advanced and the arms are placed parallel to the body touching the thighs. The facial characteristics are stylised. These statues are mainly of monumental size, but miniature kouroi have also been found. It has been suggested that the earlier kouroi were supposed to be cult statues representing Apollo, which were gradually established as sculptural types.

Libation
The offering of liquids (such as wine or milk), which were poured on the ground in the honour of a god or hero.

Metal-working
Techniques for making bronze statues:
a) Solid bronze technique. A prototype was made of wax and covered with a clay mould, over which molten bronze was poured.
b) the lost wax technique. A core almost in the dimensions of the statue was made of material which perished after the bronze was poured. The core was covered with a layer of wax, which was as thick as the final statue was going to be. On this model the details were carved. On top of

the core a clay cover was fixed with nails. The wax was melted and replaced by bronze. The limbs and additional details were worked separately and attached at the final stage.

Metope
A stone slab of rectangular or square shape, which was usually decorated in relief. The metopes were part of the Doric frieze and alternated with triglyphs.

Monopteros
A temple-shaped building, often circular, with an exterior colonnade, and without a cella in the interior.

Oikos
A rectangular building with a small entrance.

Opisthodomos
The rear part of a temple, which is usually oriented to the west.

Palaestra
Building used for exercising and teaching. It is usually arranged with rooms around a central courtyard.

Pediment
The triangular part carried by the entablature on the front and the back of temples or temple-shaped buildings.

Peribolos
The wall marking the boundaries of a temenos. It was built around the temples and the offerings of a sanctuary.

Peripteros
A temple surrounded by an exterior colonnade.

Perirrhanterion
A shallow vessel, usually made of marble, supported on female statues which are standing next to lions or are stepping on lions. It originated either in the East or in the islands.

Pronaos
The front porch of a temple, usually oriented to the east.

Prostyle
A temple with a row of columns in front of the cella (e.g. the temple of Athena Pronaia of the 4th century BC).

Pteron
The exterior colonnade around the walls of a cella.

Retaining wall
A solid stone structure, supporting buildings and other structures built on slopes.

Stele (pl. stelai)
A stone slab used for sculptured reliefs or for inscriptions; tombstone.

Stoa
A long and narrow building with a colonnade at the front. It was used as a place for storage, exhibition, or trade, and was usually located in sanctuaries or agorai (fora).

Strigil
A metallic object of ellipsoid shape, used by athletes for scrubbing off the oil, which they spread on their bodies before exercising at the palaestra.

Temenos
The geographical limits of a sacred area dedicated to a specific deity.

Tholos
A circular peripteral building.

Treasury
A temple-shaped building of small scale, which was usually prostyle, or with two columns *in antis*. It could be dedicated by a city to panhellenic sanctuaries, such as Delphi and Olympia.

Triglyph
The decorative part between two metopes on a Doric frieze.

Tripod
A base with three feet which was used to support vessels without a foot, such as cauldrons.

Two columns in antis
Type of temple with two columns between the antae formed at the end of their long walls.

Epilogue

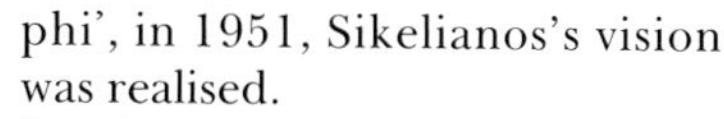

"...There, since early times, religious motivation was freed from any strong fanaticism and was expressed as an international henotheism above any dogmatic polytheism or dogmatic monotheism, where all human spirits could be encountered and embraced not only beyond mountains and seas, but also beyond the deep differences of language, custom, cult and law. That was the spirit which led Delphi to take over the education of the Greek nation on the one hand and to attempt, through its general glory, to break down the boundaries which separated countries and people. With this spirit from early antiquity Delphic unity embraced the East and the West, exactly as the two eagles sent off by Zeus from the opposite ends of the world found a nest together on the Delphic rock, which is called the omphalos of the earth. This rock indicated the spiritual centre of the earth...."

***The Delphic Association* Angelos Sikelianos**

With these words Angelos Sikelianos describes his idea to establish Delphi as the intellectual capital of Europe. The history and the imposing landscape of Delphi enchanted the famous Greek poet and inspired him to introduced the so-called Delphic Idea in 1924. His objective was to revive the glory and the cosmopolitan character of Delphi by bringing together leading figures in the arts and literature and by founding a University. The fulfilment of Sikelianos's dream began with the performance of two ancient tragedies at the ancient theatre of Delphi: the *Prometheus Bound* in 1927 and the *Suppliants* in 1930, both written by Aeschylus. Unfortunately, the poet did not live long enough to see his dream come true, but with the foundation of the 'European Cultural Centre of Delphi', in 1951, Sikelianos's vision was realised.

The closing of the Delphic oracle after the establishment of Christianity sealed a long chapter in the history of ancient Greek religion. The sanctuary was indeed literally sealed when the modern village of Castri was built on top of the architectural remains and the offerings at the site. Delphi ceased to be a religious and educational centre. The fame of Delphi was revived many years later by the French excavations which brought to light valuable finds. Historians were impressed both by the religious importance of the site and by its political and social significance. The idea of the Delphic Amphictyony excited the European nations so profoundly because it was considered to constitute a message of peace, reconciliation and unity and because it represented a prototype for European civilisation.

Today, Delphi is a spiritual and cultural centre, although the idea of Angelos Sikelianos was never fulfilled as it had been originally conceived. The archaeological finds, however, are the living proof of the glory and the importance of the site which has not died out and never will throughout the centuries. The visitor approaching Delphi from the road from Arahova faces a magnificent view. First the sanctuary of Apollo comes into sight, dominated by the remaining standing columns of the temple of Apollo and the treasury of the Athenians, while on the left side of the road the very impressive tholos is visible in the sanctuary of Athena Pronaia. It is a unique view, as the imposing volumes of the buildings can be seen between the mountain tops and the sea in the background– a view that everyone should experience, particularly against the colours of the setting sun.

Amandry, P.,	La mantique apollonienne à Delphes (1950)
Andronikos, M.,	Delphi (1992)
Bommelaer, J.-F.	Guide de Delphes. Le site (École Française d' Athènes, 1991) Guide de Delphes. Le musée (École Française d' Athènes, 1991)
Bouquet, J.,	La destination de la Tholos de Delphes (1960)
Burkert, W.,	Greek Religion (1985)
Bommelaer, J.-F., (ed.),	Centenaire de la «Grande Fouille» réalisée par l' école Française d' Athènes (1892-1903). Actes du Colloque Paul Perdrizet. Strasbourg, 6-9 November 1991 (1992)
European Cultural Centre	Symposium, "The Delphic Idea and Europe" Delphi, May 25-27, 1978 (European Cultural Centre of Delphi, 1979)
Kakrides, I. Th. (ed.)	Greek Mythology, vol. 1-5 (1986) (in Greek)
Karouzos, Ch.,	Delphi (1974)
Keramopoulos, A.,	The topography of Delphi (1917)
Nilsson, M.,	History of Ancient Greek Religion (1963)
Papachatzis, N. D.,	Religion in Ancient Greece (1987) (in Greek)
Papachatzis, N. D.,	Pausanias, Description of Greece, Boeotia and Phokis. Books 9 and 10 (1981) (in Greek)
Parke, H. W.,	Greek Oracles (1977)
Parke, H.W., and Wormell, D.E.W.,	The Delphic Oracle (1956)
Petrakos, B.,	Delphi (1977)
Roux, G.,	Delphes, son oracle et ses dieux (1976)
Themelis, P. G.	The Museum of Delphi (1981)
Tsoura, A.,	Arahova, Corycian Cave of Parnassos. (1992) (in Greek)

ARTISTIC SUPERVISION: KOSTAS ADAM
GREEK TEXT: MARILENA CARABATEA
ENGLISH TRANSLATION: MARILENA CARABATEA
MAPS AND DRAWINGS: STELIOS DASKALAKIS
LAY-OUT: CHRISTE KASASTOGIANNI
PHOTOGRAPHS:GIANNIS GIANNELOS, KOSTAS ADAM
MONTAGE-PRINTING-BINDING: PERGAMOS S.A.